The
WRITING
on the
Classroom
Wall

How Posting Your Most Passionate
Beliefs about Education Can Empower
Your Students, Propel Your Growth,
and Lead to a Lifetime of Learning

Steve Wyborney

The Writing on the Classroom Wall
©2016 by Steve Wyborney

This book is available at special discounts when purchased in quantity for use as premiums, promotions, fundraisers, or for educational use. For inquiries and details, contact the publisher at shelley@daveburgessconsulting.com.

Published by Dave Burgess Consulting, Inc.
San Diego, CA
http://daveburgessconsulting.com

Cover Design by Genesis Kohler
Author photo by Robin Wheeler
Editing and Interior Design by My Writers' Connection

Library of Congress Control Number: 2016936794
Paperback ISBN: 978-0-9969895-0-3
Ebook ISBN: 978-0-9969895-1-0

First Printing: May 2016

"Steve shares his personal and authentic method of transparency with his students in this reflective book. His words are an inspiration for all educators to pursue the same passion and transparency within their classroom, school, and community. Steve promotes the importance of having a strong, healthy culture of learning and details his journey in making that a reality in his own profession. This book is a must read for all educators."

—*Bethany Hill, lead learner/principal, Cabot, Arkansas*

"Engaging students in global conversation and promoting positive sharing is my passion. In this book, Steve Wyborney clarifies many ideas and shares many more that will directly impact the way I teach, share, and contribute to the wider education community. Thanks for inspiring me, Steve."

—*Craig Kemp, New Zealand-born international educator, head of technology integration, speaker, and co-founder of #WhatIsSchool and #asiaed*

"Powerful and easy to connect with, Steve Wyborney's new book emphasizes a classroom where everyone is a teacher and a learner. This is a book that will not only give you ideas and answers but will leave you asking questions, which is the same type of learning that Steve models in his own classroom. The more books focused on *learning* in education, the better off we are."

—*George Couros, author of The Innovator's Mindset*

"Every new teacher should read *The Writing on the Classroom Wall* to refresh the brain about what learning, writing, and making connections is all about!"

—*Eric Jensen, author of Teaching with the Brain in Mind*

"Part inspiration, part specific classroom strategies, this book pushes teachers to place the most important ideas in front of students every day. Each chapter contains motivation to improve and a guiding set of questions to ensure that your teacher skill set will improve."

—*Jeff Charbonneau, 2013 National Teacher of the Year*

"In *The Writing on the Classroom Wall*, Steve breaks down big ideas and shares the tools needed to step outside of your comfort zone and take risks. Follow Steve's lead and put your beliefs out there. It's a leap worth taking!"

—*Todd Nesloney, White House Champion of Change, two-time Bammy Award recipient, co-founder of #KidsDeservelt, principal at Webb Elementary, Navasota, Texas*

DEDICATION

To Ernie Thompson,
with deep respect, admiration, and appreciation

CONTENTS

PREFACE

I am deeply grateful for the numerous educators, friends, family members, and others who have influenced my personal growth journey. While I will attempt to detail helpful parts of that journey here, I cannot do so without acknowledging how our lives overlap and, in the process, fuel one another's growth. As you read this book, our journeys will begin to intertwine.

In this book, you may encounter new ideas. Likewise, you may recognize some ideas that have been widely discussed. My intent is to share—with both clarity and urgency—some of the best ideas and practices I have benefited from during my journey as an educator.

My hope is that if these ideas are new to you, you will consider them deeply. And if some of these ideas have already occurred to you, I encourage you to contemplate them in a new light.

Perhaps some of the value of these ideas lies in the words themselves, many of which have been given to me as bits of wisdom by other educators in my life. However, the greatest value for you might be in the simple sense of permission—the permission to discover, identify, and post profound ideas on the wall of your classroom.

When you do, please share them with me. I would love to hear what inspires you—and I would deeply value your insights. One of the Big Ideas in this book is "When You Discover Something New, Design a Path That Can Be Followed." Here is my path.

I am looking forward to learning about your Big Ideas!

All the best,
Steve

INTRODUCTION

My desire is to make an impact on classrooms around the world with this book. I fully realize the boldness of that statement, but I am willing to risk it—now. Until a year ago, it would not have occurred to me that such an impact was possible. My scope of vision expanded, however, when I discovered Twitter in 2014 and started a blog later that same year. At first, I saw the blog purely as an opportunity to learn. In fact, I titled it "I'm on a Learning Mission." After eleven months, my blog had been visited by educators and other readers from 120 countries. I learned that there is a large and growing body of globally connected educators who regularly impact one another's practice.

Today, I frequently converse with educators around the world through my blog and on Twitter. Those men and women contribute to my craft and my thinking on a daily basis, a gift for which I am tremendously grateful. I am also grateful for the new understanding of the potential scope and scale of any educator's impact. I now clearly see that any educator can influence, help, and support his or her peers around the globe.

If you have yet to access the growing community of connected educators around the world, I encourage you to take the step. It can feel like a risk, I know. For me, it was a step I had never considered. Then, the idea of connecting through social media intrigued me. Now, I stand amazed at the power of the community and the stream of learning that is there for me to access and take in at whatever pace I choose. As part of that community, I have learned that one of the best ways for me to learn is to share. In fact, I learn best by sharing the ideas and insights I have picked up along the way, which brings us to this book. I would like to reach back into my journey as an educator and *risk forward* by sharing *The Writing on the Classroom Wall.*

The Space on Your Wall

There is an opportunity on your wall right now. It is a powerful opportunity for both you and your students.

If you look around your room, you will see it: a blank space on your wall that is waiting for you to post your deepest, most passionate beliefs about learning. This space is waiting to be filled with a message that summarizes your mission, your passion, and your core beliefs about learning.

This space will also challenge you. It may cause you to grapple with your beliefs about teaching and learning. And if you embrace the opportunity, it will also reveal important questions. It is a space that, once filled with your message, will allow you to share messages with students that will deeply impact their lives, empower their hunger to learn, and propel them forward as a classroom community.

It took me years to discover the first blank space on my wall and even longer to understand its importance and potential. That simple discovery changed who I was as a teacher and as a person.

The blank space on your wall—which you may already be visualizing—is a prime opportunity for you. I challenge you to take hold of that opportunity and fill it with possibilities.

If you take the risk, it will impact your students.

It will also have a profound impact on you, both personally and professionally.

It's right there. It's waiting for you.

Do you see it? The space on your wall.

The Journey Begins

In the fall of 1997, I taped a simple message on the wall of my classroom. It was only five words long, but those five words launched me on a profound journey. As I stood back and looked at the words on the wall, and as I anticipated explaining their true meaning to the students, I had no idea that they held a much deeper meaning for myself.

Nor did I have any idea that I would soon be posting other messages on the classroom wall. I did not see that I was at the beginning of a journey I would cycle through again and again, at increasingly deeper levels, over the course of my career, each time realizing a more substantial meaning to the truths I continued to post. But those first, simple words gave me the courage to post other messages, including what I ultimately realized to be the most powerful, profound truth about students I have ever encountered.

My journey was not a rapid one, nor was it without its setbacks. Some seemingly powerful ideas I posted fell flat with students. Even as I took those particular ideas down, I grew from my experiences with them. I continued to learn, year after year and with each newly posted message. Several years later, as I taped up the fourteenth message, my understanding about students reached a profound clarity. That was when I knew I needed to share my learning beyond the walls on which the messages were taped.

While I could have stopped at the fourteenth message, the truth is that my hunger to grow constantly drove me forward. Through my years as an educator, I've become passionate about seeking out powerful truths regarding students and classrooms. I now realize I will never complete my pursuit of learning. Like so many other educators around me, I have a passion to grow, to continue learning, and to constantly reflect. So the messages continued to grow, and the writing stretched farther and farther across the wall.

My personal journey as an educator causes me to reflect often, and the most profound reflections speak important truths to both my students and myself. Those are the reflections I post, the ones I explain, and the ones I reference in the thick of instruction. They are also the thoughts shared in *The Writing on the Classroom Wall*.

I invite you to join me on a journey that I have lived out for years. As you read, I encourage you to consider the messages and post one (or more) of them on the wall of your classroom, inviting your students to fully appreciate what those words mean to you. Or, even better, I invite you to reflect on what you deeply believe as an educator and on the message you recognize as an important truth for your students to hear. Then, post *that* writing on the wall in your classroom.

Slow Bolts of Lightning

Epiphanies. I've noticed that they often wait for ideal conditions before they strike. And sometimes it takes years for those conditions to develop. I call such epiphanies "slow bolts of lightning." Although I may have agreed with an idea prior to its revelation in my life, the experiences of my career had simply not prepared me to begin to recognize the weight of that particular truth. Many of the readying conditions that prepared me for these slow bolts of lightning were found in my classroom, within the interactions with students, and in the many moments of reflection in which I contemplated, learned, and grew as an educator.

Almost every time an epiphany strikes, I marvel at how I had ever missed its truth. Often, it is an idea has that has been repeatedly poured into my life or a truth that has been standing in front of me for years. Suddenly, what may have been a vague, peripheral concept is clear and obvious. I am not the originator of these ideas; I have merely recognized their validity and power and have been deeply impacted by them. I hope at least one of these bolts finds its mark in your life.

CHAPTER 1
THE HOLE IN OUR
CONVERSATION AND THE
SPACE ON OUR WALL

Three years into my teaching career, I was struck by an awkward realization—a slow bolt of lightning. I realized that there was a profound question I had never posed to my students. The question was probably one of the most relevant and important questions I could ask in the midst of a learning community, yet I had completely overlooked it. The truth was that it hadn't even occurred to me.

And then the realization struck me.

In a moment of revelation, it occurred to me that the one thing we seldom talked about—in the midst of our learning community—was learning itself.

We were a classroom community where learning was taking place. In fact, the purpose of the classroom was to be a place of learning. Yet we had never dared to ask the questions: What is learning? How can we learn about learning itself?

I had always expected my students to learn. I provided them with strategies to learn. However, I had not taught them what it meant to learn. I had been relying on an assumption that learning was what happened at school, and since we all knew that, there was no need to learn about learning itself. After all, we had all been learning our entire lives.

As the teacher, standing in the middle of a learning community, this was a stunning realization.

The conditions had become ripe, and I was struck by the first of many slow bolts of lightning. It had taken nearly three years to develop.

Beginning to Grapple

I immediately began wrestling with the question, "What is learning?"

I found the question to be simultaneously very simple and quite complex. It is also highly personal. Perhaps the complexity of the question is why it is rarely approached. However, we were a learning community, so it seemed to be very important to address this question.

So that is what I set out to do.

I began an unexpected journey, one that I was utterly unprepared to comprehend.

As I pursued the question of how to frame the concept of learning for my students, it quickly became apparent to me that learning is nearly always rooted in ideas or contexts that are either existing or in formation. On one hand, this made the concept simple. On the other hand, due to the wide variety of contexts, personal experiences, and their ongoing fluctuating development, the idea of learning was also very complex.

After deeply wrestling with how to begin approaching the subject with my students, I arrived at a simple statement that I had heard several times before, one that I now saw in a new light.

I wrote it down and posted it on the wall.

BIG IDEA 1
Learning Is about Making Connections.

I had no idea how powerful this statement truly was, but it was succinct and seemed to encompass the wide variety of contexts and paradigms that we all brought into the classroom.

The next day, I shared the idea with the students and explained to them what it meant. I detailed that much of our learning is about connecting ideas. Sometimes we compare, but other times we contrast. I did my best to reach to a student level to explain that we root new ideas within a context, or a framework, or a paradigm that already exists, and in doing so we grow that context so that it can accommodate even more learning.

Sometimes we find ideas that conflict with each other. Recognizing those conflicts is another way of making a connection. Not all connections fit together smoothly. Sometimes the connections don't seem to make sense.

- If three is less than four, why isn't one-third less than one-fourth?
- Why do we fight for peace?
- How can we describe a reaction as both opposite and equal?

When we struggle to make connections that do not seem to make sense, we are on the brink of powerful learning. Those moments of dissonance are especially important because they call us to deeper questions and stronger learning. So instead of rejecting connections that don't seem to make sense, let's prize those connections. Instead of deciding that points of confusion conflict with learning, let's understand that those points of confusion actually provide some of the richest opportunities to learn.

Sometimes we find several correct options, and so we find vantage points, and we find perspective. That can give us choices and allow us to see things through the eyes of other learners in our community. We can connect those vantage points to discover greater perspectives. When we begin to look through the eyes of others, we can value their ideas and also begin to understand that our own ideas can impact those around us. When we recognize that our ideas have the potential to contribute to the lives of others, we are called upon to articulate our ideas clearly so they can meaningfully become part of the connections made by others.

We learn that the nature of learning itself is complex and that making connections is not always easy. Sometimes the connections are very apparent. Sometimes the teacher illuminates the connections for us. Yet it is so much more powerful if we actively search for and make our own connections. We are learners. We are connectors. Learning is about making connections and that is something that we do, not something that someone else does for us.

The concept was immediately powerful. I had no idea what I had just started.

The simple concept of making connections established a common paradigm for us to communicate within. While my thoughts around learning itself were becoming clearer, I was also learning from the students who quickly offered examples of making connections, using ideas that were relevant to them, using examples that made it more real to our classroom community, using examples that truly connected our classroom community.

How the Idea Grew

And then the Big Idea on the wall stunned me with an additional meaning. The deeper truth. The one that I should have recognized all along. While it was entirely true that learning is about making content connections in the very way that I had intended, a much more profound truth was emerging from those five simple words. It had been staring at me for many months before it finally occurred to me.

Learning is about making connections. While this describes the nature of learning, it also points toward a fundamental, primary truth of classroom life. The most important connections that can be made in any classroom are the relationships.

Building relationships is essential.

Teachers who invest in relationships empower students.

The reason that our learning was able to travel into the territory of taking risks, sharing ideas, and seeking connections was not simply because we had discussed the concept of learning. It was something much greater. The reason our classroom community was traveling with momentum was that we were building powerful relationships.

It was clear that building relationships with students was absolutely foundational to all of the learning that followed. Rapport with students is critical. A teacher who never connects with students will never build a powerful classroom culture.

The truth had been staring at me from the wall for months before I was ever struck with the deeper meaning. Learning is about making connections—with students.

Building relationships with students is one of the most critical and most powerful attributes of effective teaching.

Taking the time to build relationships with students comes in the form of listening carefully and striving to understand. It comes in the form of sharing who you are and being transparent about your own learning journey and experiences, which is a powerful point of connection.

Powerful learning rests on powerful relationships. Learning is about making connections.

KEY QUESTIONS

1. Have you asked your students, "What is learning?"

2. How would they respond? How would you answer the question?

3. What does "Learning Is about Making Connections" mean to you?

4. Why are relationships such an important part of a learning community?

CHAPTER 2
MOMENTUM

S oon after posting "Learning Is about Making Connections," I sensed the power of posting a Big Idea, and felt the need to identify additional Big Ideas. However, I had not yet traveled enough of a reflective journey to sense what the next Big Idea might be. Even so, I felt the need for an example that I could quickly reference. I needed something that could help to further ground the concept of connections.

I posted an idea that featured what I assumed to be a very simple connection.

BIG IDEA 2
ADDITION AND SUBTRACTION
ARE CONNECTED.

Introducing the Big Idea

"Girls and boys, we know that learning is about making connections. I'd like to give you an example. Addition and subtraction are connected."

Then I proceeded to write a graphic on the board that has been used in many classrooms far and wide.

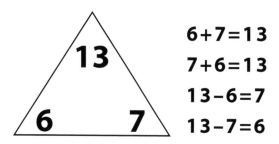

*"We can see here how addition and subtraction are connected. This is an idea that you learned years ago, but our Big Idea is that learning is about **making** connections. Let's find out more. Let's make some connections."*

And with that, I launched into a series of questions.

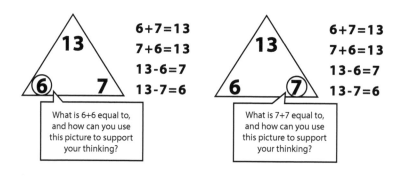

Seeking more connections, we began exploring the relationships among all three numbers. I offered more questions to the students.

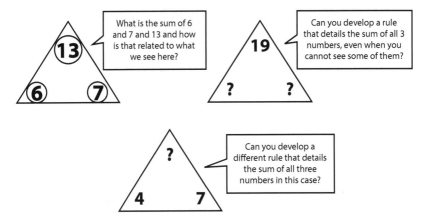

We also began exploring what may or may not be true.

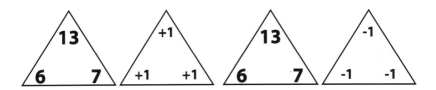

"If we add one to every number in the triangle, will the relationships stand? Why or why not? What if we subtract one from every number in the triangle? Will those relationships be true? Why or why not?"

Learning is about making connections, so we dug even deeper.

"What if we only change two numbers in the triangle? Are there any cases in which we can add one to two of the numbers in the triangle and maintain a valid relationship? Does this also work with subtraction? What does that tell us about how addition and subtraction are connected?"

Then I presented another question that earlier might have simply produced a number, but we were looking much deeper at this point.

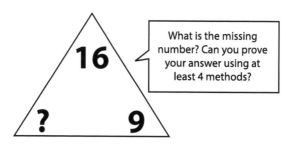

The Big Idea, coupled with the graphics, helped us to see more clearly how learning is about making connections. Admittedly, the relationship between addition and subtraction was not a profound idea that was destined to deeply impact our classroom culture. Yet the context was extremely useful. The example helped us to understand that learning connections are abundant, available, and within reach. It also helped us to recognize the importance of looking a little deeper to find those connections.

Most importantly, our pursuit of connections changed the atmosphere in the classroom. Seeking unexpected connections was empowering and invigorating. We began to hunger for those connections.

How the Idea Grew

Of the many, many lessons that my students continued to teach me, one very useful lesson was that there is great power in simply posting an image alongside a question. There is great value in allowing the opportunity which that question provides to remain available to students over the course of many days, weeks, or even months.

Instead of erasing images, I began sketching them on pieces of paper and posting them in places where students could think about them. I might post an image exactly like this, with a simple statement, such as, "I'm interested in how doubling and halving are related to this image."

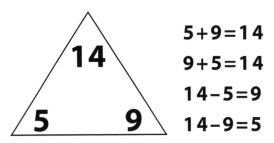

$$5+9=14$$
$$9+5=14$$
$$14-5=9$$
$$14-9=5$$

I learned that there is great power in letting opportunities linger. Allowing opportunities to linger invites wonder and insight.

With images positioned where they could tantalize the students' curiosity, we traveled through the day. Sometimes those images remained dormant for hours or days. At other times, they sprung to life as students responded to them.

> I learned that there is great power in letting opportunities linger.

When I look back on Big Idea 2, an idea which I nearly took off the wall later, I now understand that its greatest contribution to our classroom community was that it started the momentum that led to a journey. It became a paving stone, leading across a largely empty wall, and it pointed toward more empty spaces.

The first Big Idea was an extremely important experience.

The second Big Idea provided the momentum that carried the journey forward.

Key Questions

1. In your grade level or content area, what is a basic example of content that could serve as a useful example for making connections?

2. What actions can you take to cause students to look for connections?

3. Why is it so powerful to let images and questions linger together?

4. What is an example of a question that you would allow to linger on the wall?

CHAPTER 3
MORE MOMENTUM

Shortly after posting Big Idea 2, I decided that it would be useful to add another example that featured how learning is about making connections.

—————— BIG IDEA 3 ——————
MULTIPLICATION AND DIVISION
ARE CONNECTED.

Introducing the Big Idea

"Boys and girls, here is our next Big Idea. Multiplication and Division are connected. This idea reminds us that learning is about making connections. It also reminds us to look for those connections. When we find new connections, we own them. They are ours because we discovered them. Our learning is stronger when we make the connections ourselves.

"Here is an example."

On the board I wrote another graphic that has long been used in many classrooms.

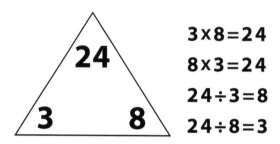

$$3 \times 8 = 24$$
$$8 \times 3 = 24$$
$$24 \div 3 = 8$$
$$24 \div 8 = 3$$

Again, I launched into a series of questions designed to cause us to seek connections and relationships.

"Learning is about making connections. Let's see what we can learn from this image. We know that multiplication and division are connected, but how can that lead us to deeper, more powerful connections?"

Then, as so often happens to all of us, the unexpected interrupted the anticipated.

"Mr. Wyborney, you also told us that repeated addition is connected to multiplication. If addition is connected to subtraction, and it's connected to multiplication, then does that mean that subtraction is connected to multiplication?" A powerful question! I began adding layers to the image, not because I knew the answer, but because I was exploring, trying to learn.

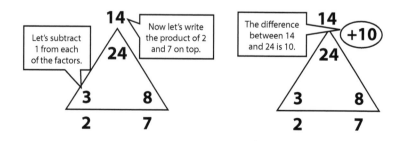

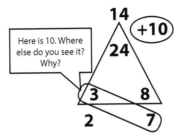

As we explored together, we found interesting connections, but we did not know if what we found were examples of something that was always true. We had made the beginning of a connection but were still grappling with how to make sense of the connection, how to attach it to our current learning.

Instead of finding an answer, we had reached a point of wondering about what might be true. We were in the process of testing a connection and wondering what it might mean. We needed more examples to help us wonder more clearly.

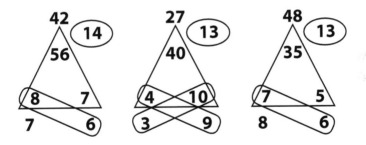

Notice how we began developing more connections and eventually began tying those connections to adding—rather than subtracting—one to each of the factors. We were primed to wonder why. We were ready to make more connections. I wanted my students to understand that connections were readily available if we pursued them. The pursuit of learning, the search for connections, and the hunt for understanding were becoming prized in our classroom.

I posted the first graphic again and restated the question: "Is subtraction related to multiplication? Let's look for connections. I want you to find the difference between all of the numbers within the triangle. Now tell me what you notice." Soon, our classroom began to look like this:

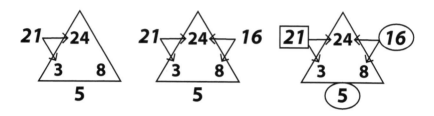

Finally, I announced: "I think this relationship may always be true. But I don't know. I think that, when we look at a multiplication fact family triangle but determine the three differences, two of those differences will always add up to the third difference." Quickly, I sketched three more examples on the board.

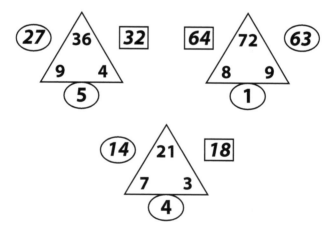

Connections are not always apparent. They do not always come quickly, and sometimes they require a great deal of wondering.

We had not reached a conclusive point of learning. Instead, we had arrived at a better place—a place of wondering.

How the Idea Grew

Again, the students saw the connections between multiplication and division, but much more importantly, they saw that many, many connections were waiting just below the surface. Those connections were within reach if we pursued them.

Perhaps most importantly, *the teacher* was beginning to make connections. I had no particular expertise with any of these ideas. I simply had a willingness to dabble and discover. My most empowering instructional move at this point was simply that I openly looked for connections myself, and I was determined to allow those connections to help me understand more about learning.

I believe the students also sensed that, while I was going to point out some examples of connections, I wasn't going to make all of the connections for them. Learning is not solely about discovering connections other people have made. It is much more than that. It is about reaching for and establishing your own connections.

Learning is an act. It is an effort. It is a deliberate choice. For us, a key part of learning was choosing to actively seek and build those connections.

This particular Big Idea grew vastly over time. In fact, its growth was part of what inspired Big Idea 17, which I'll detail later. Big Idea 3 was meant to be an example that allowed us to gain a foothold on the idea of seeking connections at deeper and deeper levels. Little did I know that it would provide such rich opportunities all on its own.

Key Questions

1. What have you noticed about how the Big Ideas are beginning to interact with one another?

2. What is a concept that you are currently teaching that has the potential for students to explore rich connections in depth?

3. How can you make those opportunities available to your students?

4. How can you make those opportunities available to yourself?

CHAPTER 4
MAKING MEANING

R eading.
What you are doing right now is an extremely powerful act. I have written these words with a specific meaning in mind. Yet you are the one interacting with the words and ideas, referencing them to your personal context and paradigms, and comparing them with many other factors. You are building layers of agreement (or disagreement), sensing possibilities, wondering what this might look like in your classroom. In doing so, you are looking at the walls of a classroom that I will likely never see. You are hearing student voices that I will likely never hear. You are visualizing, interpreting, contemplating, and conducting myriad other acts associated with the wonder of reading.

In short, you are making meaning, and while the content provides a common context for social, shared thinking, it is also a highly personal act.

Reading is thinking. Reading is about making meaning.

That is precisely what I posted next.

BIG IDEA 4
READING IS ABOUT MAKING MEANING.

Introducing the Big Idea

"Girls and boys, we will never stop learning about reading. I will point to this Big Idea often, possibly every single day. For now, I want you to understand that when we are reading, we are making meaning. That act of making meaning is not something that just happens on its own. When we read, we are extremely active thinkers who are purposefully making meaning. Making meaning is intentional. It is complicated and beautiful. I am excited to learn more about this idea."

How the Idea Grew

Reading is a complex, powerful, and important act of thinking. Reading is not isolated to the moments when our eyes are sweeping across layers of text, or story, or other representations of meaning.

Sometimes the power of reading is found in between those moments, when the student simply says, "hmmm…" and her eyes drift away from the text in deep thought about the ideas that are churning. Sometimes the power of reading is found the next day, or the next week, or even years later when she actually sees "two roads diverge" and wonders a little more deeply about the choices each one might lead to.

Reading is thinking on many, many levels. It is a powerful simultaneous interaction of multiple layers of thought, skill, content, and perception, producing meaning that we can further contemplate and appreciate.

The intention of the idea was to point out that when we read, we are to take action, to actively make meaning from the text that relates to us personally. However, what we found instead was complete permission to think very deeply about our own thinking as we read.

This concept redefined what a "strong reader" might be. A "strong reader" was an active participant who willingly and thoughtfully interacted with ideas in increasingly powerful and insightful ways.

We had just captured an enormous idea, and it had set us free to look for powerful connections.

KEY QUESTIONS

1. Have you specifically asked your students what it means to read?

2. If you asked your students, "What is reading?" how would they respond?

3. What characteristics of reading would you like your students to deeply understand and interact with?

4. What are some deliberate actions that powerful readers take during the process of reading?

CHAPTER 5
THINKING IN VIEW

One of my favorite terms early in my career, was "prewriting." What a powerful concept! To me, this meant taking time to organize and arrange thoughts in order to meaningfully prepare before the actual act of writing. To my understanding, prewriting was an important part of a process that eventually led to drafting, revising, and publishing.

Through the years, I gathered a range of prewriting strategies, including ways to use Venn Diagrams, variations of KWL charts,[1] and many other graphic organizers. These tools proved useful in our classroom, and I was intrigued by the way they provided students with access to opportunities to write.

Unfortunately, as I guided my students through a detailed writing process, I often found that the funnel of creativity seemed to narrow. The open-ended power of prewriting seemed to cultivate curiosity and creativity, and then the rest of the writing process seemed to mow it down to an unwanted uniformity.

---

1 The acronym KWL stands for What I **Know, Want** to know, and **Learned.**

To try to understand why this happened, I wrote. I wrote and wrote and wrote some more. As I wrote, I deliberately paid very careful attention to both my writing and my thinking, and I eventually reached several moments of clarity.

"Prewriting," I realized, did not take place before writing. Prewriting was not preparing to write. *Prewriting was actually writing.* Initially, I thought the different forms of prewriting, tasks that ranged from sketches, to notes, to drafts, all shared a common feature: the recording of thoughts. Even though, on a writing process timeline, prewriting would appear earlier than most other steps, the prewriting was an actual recording of thoughts. This, I concluded, was writing.

Imagine my surprise when I decided to struggle with the phrase, "recording thoughts." My initial paradigm was that the writer had a thought and then wrote it down. According to that paradigm, the writer was simply recording thinking.

As I continued to write and to work with students, I eventually realized that the act of writing involves a massive intrapersonal exchange of thinking. The refinement of thinking is spurred on by recording thoughts (in any form), and those recorded thoughts, which may come in micro-moments, continually fuel and inform the thinking.

Writing does not happen *after* thinking. Writing fuels thinking, accelerates thinking, generates thinking, is thinking, and leads to more and deeper thinking.

That discovery broke my concept of writing wide open. Finally, I understood that writing was a visible act of thinking. Perhaps most profoundly, I realized that the students' internal thinking interacted with the visibility of the thinking on the paper. In other words, writing itself helped my students write and think more clearly and creatively.

Writing consists of much more than simply recording thought; it *amplifies* thought. Writing fuels the examination of thinking—a process that includes refining, reflecting, and adapting.

Question 1 at the end of the chapter asks, "Why is writing so powerful?" If you take a moment to write an answer to that question, while simultaneously paying attention to your thinking as you write, you will notice how rapidly you interact with your words and thoughts as you process them when they land on the page. As you struggle to reach a meaning that you evaluate as satisfactory and continue to wonder about the question, you will experience the massive exchange of personal thinking that occurs during the writing process.

Writing is extraordinarily powerful!

No wonder I felt such a sense of dissatisfaction as I guided the students toward mowed-down creativity that yielded highly similar products. I was failing to acknowledge an extraordinary process.

> Writing does not happen after thinking. Writing fuels thinking, accelerates thinking, generates thinking, is thinking, and leads to more and deeper thinking.

Furthermore, when I began to understand that writing was such a powerful, massive intrapersonal exchange of thinking, I saw no reason not to unleash it in all subject areas. How could I contain something as dynamic and potent as writing to simply a "writing class?"

Phrases like, "I'd like to see all desks cleared off," didn't make sense to me anymore. Instead this made sense: "I want pencils within reach at all times." During a math lesson, I would say, "Let's write." Social studies, "Let's write." Science, "Let's write."

So, I posted the next Big Idea.

BIG IDEA 5
WRITING IS ABOUT MAKING MEANING.

Introducing the Big Idea

"Boys and girls: Writing! It's one of the most powerful actions you can take! When I wrote this Big Idea, an enormous amount of thinking happened before I ever made a mark on the page. While I was writing it, I was thinking more. And now that I can see what I wrote, my mind is thinking even more. Writing unleashes multiple layers of thinking.

"A class that is rich in writing is rich in thinking. I'd like our classroom to be very rich!

"Writing is far more than putting existing ideas on paper. Writing is about the ongoing making of ideas, the sorting of ideas, the opportunity to look at our very thoughts. Writing is about making meaning. We don't write after we finish thinking. As we write, we set our minds free to make more meaning than we had ever known was possible when we started. When we write, we invite our minds to make meaning."

My concept of writing will continually change over time. I am certain of it, because I intend to keep writing and to pay attention to what I learn from those experiences. The best way to constantly update my understanding of the power of writing is to continually write.

Resisting the Temptation to Make Meaning

As a teacher, I find that there is an unusually strong temptation to try to "make meaning for the students" by talking. Yet when I compare any attempt to "make meaning for the students" to the power of student writing, I have a difficult time making sense of any approach in which I spend a majority of the lesson talking.

One person talking—especially if it is the teacher—is not an effective means of teaching. In that scenario, the teacher, who is taking the role of the primary producer of thought and language, will have some opportunities to learn, but the students will have very few opportunities to truly learn because learning requires discovery, actively producing meaning, and making connections. In contrast, when lessons are filled with multiple opportunities for students to write and experience the massive intrapersonal exchange of thinking that writing promotes, the lesson takes on an entirely different nature.

I am learning to resist the temptation to make meaning *for* the students. I am learning to remove my voice from the conversation and to provide space for the students to be the makers of meaning. One of the best ways I have found to do that is to provide them with ample space to write.

That space, it turns out, is not difficult to find. It is especially abundant when we realize writing doesn't have to be time-consuming. In fact, powerful writing can come in short bursts.

Consider the difference between a lesson dominated by teacher-talk and another lesson about the same topic that includes multiple one-to two-minute bursts of writing. If you were to look around the classroom in the latter example, you'd see all of the students writing during several points throughout the lesson. You might notice that students are thinking, personally interacting with the content, producing ideas, and striving to make meaning. They are making connections. This lesson is focused on the same content, with one small but very powerful adaptation. The teacher has intentionally committed to providing space for student writing.

The Power of Writing and Reflecting

As a teacher, when I see the words "Writing Is about Making Meaning," I am reminded of the power of reflection. Reflection is an opportunity to allow myself to learn from my experiences and to revisit some of the thoughts I have only partially processed. Writing allows me to scratch (and sometimes claw) my way into an opportunity to more thoroughly process ideas that otherwise would not have had space or time to more fully develop.

Several of the Big Ideas in this book are drawn directly from deep, ongoing reflection. Reflective writing is a powerful process that provides opportunities to personally, deeply wrestle with thoughts and ideas that are struggling to become more fully formed.

One of the greatest benefits of committing to reflective writing is that it allows you to discover the power of reflection. When you write, you interact with your thinking, your experiences, and the representations of those experiences as they flow onto the page. As you begin to

> Reflective writing is a powerful process that provides opportunities to personally, deeply wrestle with thoughts and ideas that are struggling to become more fully formed.

go to deeper and deeper levels in your thinking, you will begin to realize that the power of this process is precisely what you want your students to experience. The rush to teach content pales in comparison to the depth and richness of learning that reflection can provide.

A fascinating aspect of reflection is that it does not have to be time-consuming. While you can commit extensive blocks of time to reflection, it is also possible to draw great power from short bursts of reflection. That reality opens up some powerful possibilities in the classroom as well. If you provide opportunities for multiple bursts of writing reflections during lessons, you may detect that students appreciate—even hunger for—the opportunities to write, to reflect, to digest, and to process the ongoing learning experience.

The life of an educator is complex, challenging, and multi-layered. We have rich and abundant learning opportunities, yet the speed of the incoming demands can easily push out the quiet moments—the opportunities for fruitful reflection.

For many educators, finding open spaces of time to reflect is a great challenge that is not easily met without a clear, strategic, intentional commitment to ongoing reflection. I have seen and experienced two successful reflection practices that you may find useful in your own endeavor to think and reflect more deeply. One is simply dedicating a block of time, often at the end of the day, to reflection. It is my intentional practice to learn more from my experiences. As my pencil hits the paper, my fingers tap the keyboard, or my voice flows into the recorder, I let myself think and interact with my thinking. I am frequently surprised and fascinated at the direction this kind reflection carries me. I make no attempt to complete the learning that reflection prompts. In truth, this time of reflection often leads to questions or thoughts that are too big to settle in a single sitting. Sometimes, I find a point of satisfaction. Other times, I uncover a deeper, unanswered question that I may want to pursue at a later time. Many times, I find both.

The other reflection tactic I use is to capture important moments, wonderings, and questions throughout the day in a rapid fashion. These are "snatches of reflection." Essentially, if I am struck by a thought, question, or wondering at any point during the day, I take a moment to capture it and stow it away.

This practice turns into rapidly sketched notes that I drop on my desk. It is not uncommon for me to find several post-it notes representing those key thoughts or questions waiting for me at the end of the day. On a few occasions, I have attempted to keep "moments of reflection" in a reflection-jotting journal, but my physical location in the classroom is unpredictable, and I'm rarely near the journal when wonder wanders my way. It's often easier to simply grab a piece of scratch paper, jot down a note, and stuff the thought in my pocket to consider later.

Perhaps I am near the front of the room, after posing a prompting question, when I feel an initial burst of audible student thinking, followed by the predictable lull that invites me to step in and fill the space with words. Yet in that moment, I know that a burst followed by a lull often leads to an even bigger burst of thinking—if I let it. So I don't interrupt. I wait for it. I bite my tongue. I know it's coming. And when it arrives, I wonder why that's so often the case. I grab a nearby sticky note and jot "Why is there a burst / lull / better burst? How do I reach the better thinking?"

Then, at the end of the day, I pull out the treasures of scratch paper, post-it notes, and torn corners and look through the questions that have captivated me throughout the day. And I write.

Writing is making meaning, and it leads me to new places. It causes me to expect and prepare for the burst of responses that fade into the lull … and then often become more reinvigorated. It causes me to wonder about what happens after the lull. Who starts to speak up? How does that opportunity to speak ignite the classroom culture? And what would happen if I gave in to the lull each time and started sharing my thoughts, instead of allowing the students to produce their own thoughts?

The practice of capturing reflective thoughts so I can consider them later reminds me where all writing begins. It starts with the intention to deliberately notice, to ask questions, to wonder, and to intentionally capture observations. It begins with choosing to reflect, choosing to respond to what we see, and choosing to make meaning.

KEY QUESTIONS

1. Why is writing so powerful?

2. How frequently are your students writing, particularly in subjects outside of language arts?

3. How can you leverage the power of writing within your lessons?

4. Instead of asking for one student to answer a question, how easy would it be for you to ask all students to respond to that question in writing?

5. What would be the effect of having all students respond in writing multiple times throughout your lesson?

6. How can you personally draw upon the power of reflection?

7. What are some strategies that you can use in the classroom to capture powerful questions for yourself?

CHAPTER 6
JOURNEYS, NOT DESTINATIONS

For many years, one of my favorite instructional tactics has been to give students a question, and in exactly the same moment, to provide students with the answer. The question and answer could be as simple as this:

What is the total?

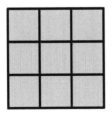 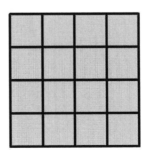

25

This strategy has always allowed me to ask questions that are far more important than the obvious. For example, "What pathways can you find that connect the question to the answer, and what can you learn from those pathways?" Then I provide space for the students to build connections between the question and the answer.

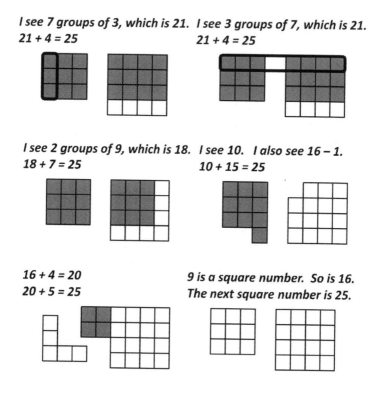

I see 7 groups of 3, which is 21.
21 + 4 = 25

I see 3 groups of 7, which is 21.
21 + 4 = 25

I see 2 groups of 9, which is 18.
18 + 7 = 25

I see 10. I also see 16 – 1.
10 + 15 = 25

16 + 4 = 20
20 + 5 = 25

9 is a square number. So is 16.
The next square number is 25.

Notice that not all of the pathways depicted above can be generalized. One of them, in particular, is not defensible. That is not a setback. In fact, it provides a powerful opportunity for further learning, by exploring if the reasoning can be generalized.

If you have not yet had a chance to use this strategy, you might feel that providing the answer to the students entirely deflates the power of the question. However, something new happens in this case: Students become free to seek important connections between the question and the answer.

More importantly, after students identify connections between the question and the answer, they go back and look for other connections. In addition, students begin to compare and contrast those connections. The comparison of connections allows for deeper understanding.

Instead of this question dead-ending at the response twenty-five, it creates space for new observations. This primes the lesson to travel to somewhere far richer than simply finding a single "right" answer.

While using this strategy, I point to a Big Idea I had posted on the wall earlier in the year, and I remember how it was introduced.

BIG IDEA 6
THERE MAY BE MANY PATHS
TO THE CORRECT ANSWER.

Introducing the Big Idea

"This is Big Idea 6: There may be many paths to the correct answer. I want you to know that when I see a question and an answer, I am only a little bit interested in the answer, especially if there is only one correct answer. Some people think finding the correct answer is the goal. Correct answers are important, but they are not very interesting. What is much, much more interesting is what we do to reach the answer. The pathway.

"The truth is that there may be many, many ways to the correct answer. There may be many pathways.

"I am a little bit interested in the correct answer, but I am VERY interested in the pathways that lead to the answer. When we find one pathway, instead of stopping there, we can look for more pathways. We can explore those pathways. We can compare those pathways. And we can see where else they lead, because they may go to some places that are far more important than the correct answer, to places that none of us were ever expecting.

"So let's start by understanding that, many times, there is not a single pathway we are all trying to follow. There may be many pathways to the correct answer. And looking for those pathways is important."

How the Idea Grew

In the quiet early morning, when I walk into the room and consider this Big Idea, I am reminded that I am only one learner among many. Although answers are important, I am compelled to validate the fact that there is rarely only one valid pathway to the correct answer. There are also invalid pathways, and even those can empower our learning.

I may enter a lesson with one pathway in mind. Yet while an obvious value exists in teaching a clear solution pathway to given situations, it is also valuable to acknowledge multiple pathways, and far more importantly, the pursuit of pathways.

The pursuit of multiple pathways to a solution, coupled with the focus on seeking connections between those pathways, empowers students to move beyond many of the original intentions of the lesson and into a discovery that makes the learning much more important.

Reaching for Personalization

Adequately personalizing a lesson for each and every student is nearly impossible when I try to contain the personalization within my own abilities. However, what is possible is empowering *students* to seek connections between the content and *their* lives.

A notable irony is that the more I try to control the personalization of the lessons, the more uniformity I create. I may even come to believe that if I rest the lesson on a topic to which I believe the students can relate, I have succeeded in personalizing the lesson. Yet if I empower the students to look for pathways, to hunt for connections, to seek how the learning intersects with their lives, *they* are much more likely to create meaningful personalization.

KEY QUESTIONS

1. Are your lessons typically focused on arriving at correct answers or on identifying multiple pathways?

2. Who is the primary producer of pathways in your classroom?

3. What are the risks of encouraging students to pursue multiple pathways?

4. What are the rewards?

CHAPTER 7
FREE TO FIND MORE

I posted the next Big Idea almost immediately after our pathways discussion.

———————— BIG IDEA 7 ————————
THERE MAY BE MANY CORRECT
ANSWERS.

Introducing the Big Idea

"Here is the next Big Idea. There may be many correct answers. We already know that there may be many pathways to the correct answer. This idea tells us even more. Sometimes there is more than one correct answer. In fact, there may be many different answers that are all correct."

Initially, this Big Idea was challenging for me to illustrate. It challenged me to find powerful questions that provided opportunities to seek richer, deeper meaning.

Rather than asking, "What is $15/20$ in lowest terms?" I asked, "What fractions are equal to $15/20$, which of those equal fractions might be most useful, and why does the usefulness of those fractions change in different situations?" The students might decide that ¾ is often useful because of its simplicity, but they would also determine that $75/100$ is sometimes a much more useful fraction. Further, they would determine that the usefulness of the numbers depends on the context in which they are being used. The students would also determine that the relationship between the numbers and the context they describe is more important than any single number I could present.

Big Idea 7 applies to more than just numbers. For example, instead of asking whether two words were synonyms or antonyms, this Big Idea allowed us to explore the richness found within the gradients of the words' meanings. We could examine the connections between words like courageous, comfortable, bold, brave, and daring to see how their meanings overlap and diverge.

The Imposter Experience

During my first year as a teacher, long before I posted any Big Ideas, I stumbled into what would become one of my all-time favorite strategies. Shortly after my fortunate stumble, I named the strategy "Imposter Sets" and have recently written a blog post about it. Although I've used this strategy for nearly twenty years, I have recently seen many variations, discovered by other educators, one of which is called "Which One Doesn't Belong?" An excellent website, also called "Which One Doesn't Belong?" (http://wodb.ca), provides many variations of this type of strategy and includes a rich and creative variety of concepts.

My personal discovery of this strategy began with a simple, poorly constructed puzzle, with a single, very limited intention.

I told the class: "Here are four numbers. One of them should not be here. It's what I call an imposter. It is posing as a number that should be in the group, but it really doesn't fit with the rest. Think about the numbers. Can you tell which one it is?"

We looked at the numbers on the board.

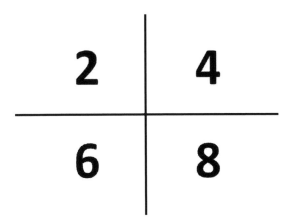

I had only one answer in mind, so I was not prepared for what was about to happen.

Not one of the students responded with my answer.

In fact, their answers were better. Although their responses sounded like guesses, they revealed important examples of reasoning.

"The two is the smallest number."

"The eight is the largest number."

"Two plus four is equal to six. So, the one that shouldn't be there is eight."

"Two times four is equal to eight. That means the six is the imposter."

"Two plus eight is equal to six plus four, so there is no imposter."

"I think it's five! Five would be right in the middle! It's five isn't it?"

I looked at the numbers on the board, wondering where the number five had come from.

"It might be twenty! They add up to twenty!"

"Yeah, and look there is a four. Twenty can be divided by four, and it would be five."

"Did you divide the twenty by that four in the picture, or did you divide it by four because there are four numbers?"

What a great question! It was one I certainly would not have thought to ask.

"I still think that five is in the middle. It's five."

Stunned—yet again—by my students, I had to admit, sheepishly, that the intended answer to my poorly-crafted question was six. I wanted to show a doubling pattern. Two doubles to four, four doubles to eight. Six was the number I thought didn't belong.

However, after that enlightening exchange, I realized that the true imposter in that scene was my very limited thinking. The students' responses opened my thinking in a way I never expected.

Right away, I wrote another set of numbers on the board, this time providing more space for multiple answers.

5	10
15	25

"Okay, this time there isn't just one answer," I began. "Some of these numbers don't fit with the rest of the set. They are the imposters. There may be different reasons why they don't fit." Although I had a few inclinations to help us begin, I also knew there could be many possibilities I had not seen yet.

"The five," I began "is the only one-digit number."

I kept looking at the numbers, sensing that there had to be more.

A student spoke up, "The ten doesn't end with a five."

"So ten isn't odd. It's the only even number," said another student.

The potential answers flowed freely now. "Five plus ten is fifteen. The twenty-five is the imposter," said one voice.

Another voice chimed in, "Yeah, but ten and fifteen is twenty-five. So the five is the imposter."

"It's ten." A quiet, seldom-heard voice captured our attention. "Look. If you add the digits together, as if they were numbers, the five is just five. The ten is a one and a zero, which adds up to one. The fifteen, if you add one and five you get six. On the twenty-five, if you add two and five the answer is seven." This shy student then went to the board and circled and wrote out the numbers so we could see her thinking process.

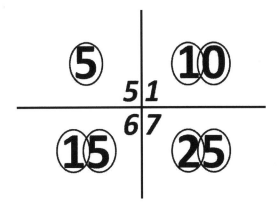

"See. Five, six, seven. They are all in a row. But the 1 doesn't fit, so ten is the imposter."

If you've never heard spontaneous applause break out in a classroom following a student response, you may never have heard the sound of a quiet, reserved student becoming publically acknowledged as a mathematician.

Once again, the classroom community had stunned me.

No longer was I embarrassed by the limitations of my initial intended answer. I had stumbled onto something far more important. It was the first taste of a truth that eventually became Big Idea 7: There may be many correct answers.

Key Questions

1. How frequently do you ask questions that feature multiple correct answers?

2. Do you promote the concept that a correct answer is not the end of the question?

3. What is the effect on students when they understand that there is more than one correct answer to a question?

4. How is the question itself impacted when students approach it with the understanding that there is more than one correct answer?

5. What are some examples of questions you could ask that would cause students to look for multiple answers?

CHAPTER 8
BUILDING

Our weekly staff meetings took place in the music room, always after the last bus had left. It was nearly time for my colleague, Bonnie, and me to give a report on the status of the *Theme Team*—a representative group of teachers working to identify a school-wide theme for the year.

As staff meetings sometimes go, it's nice to mix things up a little bit once in a while, and that was exactly what Bonnie and I had in mind that day.

The voice traveled down the agenda. "Okay, Theme Team. You're up. What's the latest?"

"Oh, that's right," I began. "We are giving a report today. We've been working on the theme for a while now. Bonnie, do we have any updates to share from the last meeting?"

Bonnie stood and smiled. "Yes, we do. The theme for this year is … " She paused dramatically before the announcement, "Under Construction!"

I turned to Bonnie. "Okay, we'll keep working on it. The theme is under construction, everyone. We'll keep working and get back to you. It might take a while."

Bonnie smiled again and shook her head. "No. You don't understand. The theme is "Under Construction." That's our theme. It's "Under Construction!"

"Ah! Nice!" floated a comment from across the room.

At this point, anyone who was not paying attention sensed either the rising conflict, the chuckles that were starting to spread around the room, or the fact that some people were noticing something ahead of others and they didn't want to be left out.

"Oh, I see!" I finally said, nodding my head. "I understand now!" Bonnie smiled, so I continued. "Everyone, the theme team is working *really hard* on the theme. It's under construction and will probably be ready any day now."

Bonnie's hands flew to her hips, but this time she didn't say anything at all—at least not with her words. She marched to the front of the room and pulled out a large sign, which she unrolled, revealing two very large words: "Under Construction."

Applause spread throughout the room.

"Well," I managed to say. "Keep working on it! Hopefully we'll be able to stand up here soon and share the theme with you. I have a feeling that it won't be long at all. And I know that I wouldn't want to miss that moment."

With that, Bonnie tossed the sign over my head and began explaining how this theme matched our school and our learners. She also shared some highly creative insights and ways the theme could be used to connect our learners throughout the school.

Our schoolwide theme that year reflected our reality. We had recently completed the construction of a new elementary school and were still working to thoughtfully define the qualities and attributes that would define our school community. It also reiterated the nature of the hard work to which we, as a learning community, felt committed.

Most importantly, it provided us with a context to share with the students about the nature of learning.

Soon after that meeting, I posted Big Idea 8.

──── BIG IDEA 8 ────
LEARNING IS CONSTRUCTION.

Introducing the Big Idea

"Girls and boys, today I would like to introduce another Big Idea! Big Idea 8 says, "Learning Is Construction." This Big Idea connects to our schoolwide theme, which is "Under Construction!" Something very important about construction—or building—is that it does not happen all at once. When something is built—like a school, or a house—there are often several layers that rely on one another. You can't build the roof until you build the walls. But you can't build the walls until after you have built the foundation. As we learn, we are often building important foundations for ideas that we will learn much later. We also need to know that what we understand right now is standing on foundations that we have already worked very hard to build.

"Learning is construction, and that causes us to think forward about the new ideas we will build. This Big Idea also causes us to think back to the ideas we are building upon."

How the Idea Grew

Learning is far more multi-layered than I had believed it to be earlier in my career. One of the most important understandings that I continue to derive from this Big Idea is that it is impossible to separate learning from the context that makes it meaningful. Learning rests on paradigms and experiences we have spent years building and organizing, and it sets the stage for future learning.

Some of the very best learning challenges our paradigms and causes them to expand or change to accommodate surprising new information.

It is true that the strength of the walls supports the roof, but it is also true that the roof protects the walls. In many ways, the roof brings new definition to the very walls upon which it rests. Likewise, learning is much more than building layer upon layer. Those layers continually redefine one another.

Unlike a construction project that eventually reaches completion, learning is not something that should see the concrete harden around the rebar. The very foundation of learning may flex and grow and change. Thankfully—impressively—our students have a stunning capacity for learning—and for growth and change. Extremely agile, our young learners continually construct and reconstruct meaning. They cause me, on an almost daily basis, to reconstruct my thinking about their deep potential and about the nature of learning itself.

Key Questions

1. How is learning similar to construction?

2. How is learning different than a construction project?

3. Have any of your students recently experienced and accommodated a substantial paradigm shift that has provided a basis for additional, unexpected learning?

4. Can you think of an example of how new learning has redefined prior learning?

5. How is your own learning under construction?

CHAPTER 9
GLAMOROUS MISTAKES

The territory of true learning is riddled with risk. Learning happens when we venture into the unknown and embrace the experience. Sometimes we will find ourselves embracing productive growth, and other times we will discover deep struggle. That's okay.

As teachers, we need to struggle. Our students need to struggle, too.

We will falter, we will make mistakes, and we will experience setbacks. Mistakes are evidence that we are pressing into new learning, that we are risking growth.

The territory of true learning
is riddled with risk.

Recently, I have heard and read a great deal about prizing failure, recognizing the opportunities found in failure, and even the necessity of failure. At the heart of this conversation is the concept that failure is often disconnected from finality. Failure is not the end. In fact, it offers new information and a new starting point. It empowers us with newly developed insight. Failure is not the goal, but it frequently turns out to be advantageous. Additionally, it may indicate that we are embracing worthwhile challenges.

To be fair, there are times when failure does include a sense of finality. Sometimes, as with failing a final exam, missing a scholarship or admissions deadline, or burning the Thanksgiving turkey as the guests are arriving, failure represents both a last chance in the moment as well as an opportunity to embrace a rich learning experience. Sometimes, it's possible to return to those specific experiences and try again. (It happens all the time at the Department of Motor Vehicles.) Other times, while we may learn from our mistakes, it is too late to try again. For example, the burnt turkey cannot be undone.

> Mistakes are gifts. They are opportunities waiting to be unwrapped.

In school, however, we rarely seek the kind of failure characterized by a combination of both finality and a complete lack of guiding feedback along the way. Instead, our aim is to press into new, challenging territory where students are highly likely to struggle, to make mistakes, to face challenges, and to grapple with new ideas. In doing so, we understand that mistakes can reveal both misconceptions and opportunities, that they can point toward partially formed, growing understandings of a challenging concept.

One of the greatest values of mistakes is that that they can immediately draw our focus to student thinking. Identifying the underlying causes of a student's misconception, for example, provides a clear window into the student's conceptual understanding which helps the teacher gather insights and reflections. Mistakes provide extremely relevant feedback. In some cases, there is no better teacher than a carefully examined mistake.

So it's important to welcome mistakes as gifts. They are opportunities waiting to be unwrapped. And when we unwrap them, we often find very useful, highly intriguing information inside. That is the point of Big Idea 9.

BIG IDEA 9
WE LEARN FROM OUR MISTAKES.

Introducing the Big Idea

"Learning is about making connections. On our way to those connections, we will make many mistakes. You will make mistakes, and I will make mistakes, too. Let's just say that all together, so nobody has to worry about trying to stay away from mistakes: **We will all make mistakes.** *They are going to come. And when they come, let's take advantage of them.*

"This might surprise you, but there is actually an enormous amount of learning that can come from making mistakes, especially when we take the time to learn from them. We can either ignore our mistakes, or we can try to learn from them.

"Since we are all going to make mistakes, and since we can learn so much from them, let's embrace our mistakes and allow them to teach us. You may be surprised at the power of the connections that come from mistakes.

"We won't try to make mistakes on purpose, but let's agree to this: We will not defend our learning against mistakes. We won't try to explain away mistakes. When we discover them, we'll see what they can teach us."

This particular Big Idea requires some extra care to unroll in the classroom. Some learners interpret this idea far differently than it is

We will not defend our learning against mistakes.

intended. Rather than a sense of freedom to learn from mistakes, some students have learned over time that mistakes serve the purpose of teaching us to never again repeat a specific failure.

For example, one morning while hurrying to get ready for school, I brushed against a hot iron. That was clearly a mistake. It was the kind of mistake that sent me a clear warning to never make the same mistake again.

Some students have had bad academic experiences with mistakes, and those mistakes have taught them to do all they can to avoid repeating those mistakes. That is *not* the concept intended by Big Idea 9.

In the classroom, mistakes are not meant to be occurrences that teach us to never make mistakes again. Rather, mistakes offer valuable information when we examine them. We may try and fail again and again, testing new theories and methods. And if we learn from the feedback of those failures, we enrich our connections and grow as learners.

How the Idea Grew

One of the wide appeals of this concept is that it communicates that perfection is not necessary. Students should own the personal freedom to not punish themselves, feel ashamed, or look down upon themselves if they make a mistake.

At its heart, the message says, "It's okay." Then it goes on to detail how it is actually advantageous to make mistakes. But that's not all. The message also gives us permission to venture into bolder, riskier territory. It provides a sense of safety within the learning community that publically communicates the greater worthiness of trying—even if trying means not succeeding for a long time.

This message is not just for students. As educators, we may feel as if we cannot afford to make any mistakes because education is so important. I would like to offer a counterpoint. Education is extraordinarily important. So as educators, we *must* step into the challenging territory of growth where we are highly likely to make mistakes. We need to press our growth journey to the point where we may frequently falter and fail—and then go on to grow from the feedback we receive.

When we recognize that we have made a mistake in front of students, we have an important decision to make. One option is to ignore it, cover it up, or quickly move past it. The other option is to point it out. "Look! I think I just made a mistake! This is a great chance for me to learn! I wonder what I can learn from it. Let's take a look at it together and see what we can find." Your modeling will set the tone for the class and will encourage students to find value in the mistakes they make.

The first option, trying to cover up a mistake, misses an opportunity, and it rarely works. Many of your students will recognize the mistake, and they will see how you handle it. Your actions will soon be reflected in their actions.

Welcome mistakes into your classroom. Then prize the thinking opportunities those mistakes provide.

KEY QUESTIONS

1. How do you communicate the value of mistakes before they happen in class?

2. How do you affirm the value of mistakes after they have occurred?

3. What do you think might be the greatest contribution that a culture of mistake-acceptance could make to a classroom?

4. How would you like your students to respond to and interact with mistakes?

CHAPTER 10
REFLECTING ON SUCCESS

Mistakes carry a sense of mystery. When we identify a mistake, we are inclined to wonder how it happened and, ultimately, what we can learn from it. Mistakes shine a spotlight on thinking, cause us to examine choices carefully, and offer a great deal of value.

Successes produce much different responses. Many successes are acknowledged and then left behind. They are less frequently examined for underlying causes or factors that contributed to the outcome, especially if the task did not produce any unanticipated thinking. The successes that do manage to draw attention include unexpected thinking, novel approaches, or unique representations of ideas.

It is clear that success needs to take a page out of failure's playbook. And that is exactly what we decided to do with the next Big Idea.

BIG IDEA 10
WE LEARN FROM OUR SUCCESSES.

Introducing the Big Idea

"We already know mistakes provide us with powerful opportunities to learn. Why is that? One of the reasons is that mistakes make us stop. They cause us to focus. They make us look at our thinking. They point out a very important idea.

"Our successes also offer powerful opportunities to learn. But just like mistakes, finding the value requires us to stop. We have to focus. We have to look carefully at our thinking.

"What is tricky with successes is that they may not encourage us to stop. They may encourage us to simply keep going without taking a close look at our thinking. But this Big Idea—We Learn from Our Successes—helps us understand that it is very important to learn from the times when we are successful, to wonder why, and to grow from those successes.

"We know that mistakes will come. We've already seen their power. But we also know that successes will come. Our successes have a lot to offer to us, too. We need to be ready for it. So this is our new Big Idea: We Learn from Our Successes."

To put this Big Idea into action in our classroom, we began to revisit our successes. One of our best strategies for revisiting successes was simply to create posters that showed the students' successes and the thinking behind them. Using large sheets of paper, my students created jumbo-sized representations of something they were proud to have accomplished—and *how* they did it. And of course, we hung those posters on the wall. While the apparent value in this practice was that thinking would be displayed around the room, an even greater value was found when students revisited their own thinking either during the *posterizing* process or when they later pointed to it during discussions and compared it to ongoing, developing ideas.

Once again, the walls were filled with opportunity.

We developed newscasts and broadcasted our thinking throughout the school, featuring multiple perspectives on math problems. I also animated a few examples of thinking for the students.

"I'm going to learn from your thinking," I told the students. "In fact, I am going to build animated representations of the thinking you share with the class. Then you can look at moving pictures of your own thinking. We will look at your successes, we will learn from those successes, and then we will see how we can connect those successes to even more learning."

This innovative practice turned out to be extraordinarily effective because it was rooted in a meaningful, authentic context: actual student thinking. It also showcased insights from which we could all learn. The most significant reason learning from our successes proved so powerful mirrored the reason that learning from mistakes is so powerful. It brought a clear focus to student thinking in such a way that it featured safe opportunities to improve and extend our learning.

There is no denying that mistakes are important experiences from which we can learn. It is also true that effectively capturing the power of mistakes and applying it to successes can produce remarkable results.

How the Idea Grew

As educators, it is easy to be reflective in the times when we falter in our lessons, when we feel as if our classroom management is slipping, or when students are having difficulty finding meaningful success. We may sense that we are making many mistakes and feel a gnawing sensation, even in the middle of a lesson, that a learning experience is simply inadequate for our students. The recognition of falling short of our hopes and desires fuels reflection. Additionally, the desire to prepare a better day spurs us on to even deeper reflection. So we take action to improve. Yearning to improve prompts reflection.

However, when the learning is strong, when the classroom community is resonating, and when we feel an intense sense of purpose, we may feel less inclined to reflect. Yet this may be the perfect time to

> Mistakes are important experiences from which we can learn.

stop and evaluate what is working and why. These successes may represent attaining some of the very goals for which we have been reaching, which makes these times of achievement very significant. This is an especially important time to take note.

Take the opportunity to reflect with clarity on your successes.

Do not waste the opportunity by asking yourself what could have been better. Do not lose your focus by asking what you could have done differently. Do not be fooled into believing that the only path to reflective growth is related to the question, "What could you have improved?"

Instead, embrace three important steps:

1. Recognize your successful experience.
2. Understand that a powerful learning opportunity exists.
3. Take advantage of that opportunity and choose to learn from your success.

Every educator enjoys a highly effective day, when things just seem to go right. Though we may feel a sense of satisfaction, too many teachers let the learning opportunity of a highly effective day pass them by. Make the choice to take a few minutes to learn from your successes. If this seems like it won't add much value, consider this: Learning from your success could lead to more great days. Likewise, you will achieve a better understanding of how you grew in your effectiveness as a teacher. Within your reflection, you may identify some surprising, important truths and strategies that you can quickly capitalize on in future classroom moments.

When you experience a great day or a momentary win, ask yourself the kinds of questions, such as those at the end of this chapter, that will help you to identify the catalysts and factors that influenced the day. Although you may be tempted to move on to the next day with very little reflection, note the power of the learning opportunity before you. Take the opportunity. Drawing value from today's success may allow you to step forward to an even greater success tomorrow.

I challenge you to learn from your successes.

Key Questions

1. Why is it often more difficult to learn from successes than from mistakes?

2. What are some of the most powerful benefits of learning from our successes?

3. What do we need to do in order to learn from our successes?

Key Questions to Contemplate following a Successful Instructional Experience

1. How did the day or lesson begin and why was that important?

2. What factors influenced your demeanor, energy level, and outlook during the day?

3. How did the students interact with one another? Why?

4. Did you face interesting pivotal points, make unique decisions, or take instructional risks during the lesson?

5. What active thinking opportunities did you provide to the students?

6. What were the students doing during the lesson?

7. Who was producing the meaning in the classroom?

8. What were you doing? What were you not doing?

9. How would you describe your anticipation of the lesson?

10. Why was today unique?

CHAPTER 11
THE POWER OF WHAT YOUR
STUDENTS ALREADY KNOW

**WARNING! This chapter is
highly counter-intuitive.
Read at your own risk!**

Hundreds of the lessons I taught in the early part of my career were built on a paradigm from which I have since broken away. As a young teacher, I defined learning opportunities as a combination of what the teacher already knew and what the students did not yet know. After all, it wouldn't make sense to teach the students what they already knew. Likewise, it wouldn't make sense to teach a lesson that I did not fully understand.

Thanks to my students, those paradigms have completely shifted.

Now, I understand that it absolutely makes sense to teach the students about what they already know. Likewise, it now makes complete sense to me to teach a lesson on a topic I do not fully understand.

The reason for my change in thinking? Today, I see far more value in dilemmas than conclusions, which means I no longer feel the need to orchestrate harmony between questions and answers. Instead, I encourage my students (and myself) to struggle with dissonance. I have much less need for the "teacher GPS" that constantly tells students, "You are at Point A, and I will completely guide you to point B. If you falter for a micro-moment, I will reroute you."

The falters in those micro-moments provide rich learning opportunities. And when students build upon the success that comes from persisting through those struggles, they experience new learning—learning that will add value to *future* learning.

Additionally, encouraging students to reach for *their* paradigms, *their* current understanding, *their* perspectives, and *their* own personal experiences—instead of mine—is a habit that promotes enormous growth.

Now it makes complete sense to ask students to reach toward what they do know, rather than simply toward what they do not know.

During the journey in the direction of this understanding, I posted the next Big Idea on the wall.

BIG IDEA 11
One of the Most Important Factors in Learning Is What You Already Know.

Introducing the Big Idea

"Many people think learning is about new ideas, new information, and new discoveries. It's true. Much of learning has to do with the new. But we also know learning is about making connections. So I have a

question. When we have those new ideas or new discoveries and when we experience that new learning, what do we attach them to? We attach learning to ideas or experiences that we already own.

"When we learn about fuchsia, we may attach it to purple. When we learn about remainders, we may attach them to fractions. When I teach you about dissonance, you may contrast it with what we already know about harmony.

"The learning you already own is extremely important. Remember that Big Idea 8 says, 'Learning Is Construction.' You have a lifetime of learning experiences. You have been learning, and learning, and learning. We will continue to experience many new ideas together in class, but I want you to understand very clearly that what you already know is very, very important. In fact, I think that what you already know may be one of the most important factors in your learning."

How the Idea Grew

Giving students opportunities to reach for what they already know is one of the best ways to help them reach for what they do not know.

Even though I had seen this reality in action many times, it took a long time for this particular slow bolt of lightning to strike. I should have recognized it in the way children watch the same movie over and over and over, each time discovering new meaning in it. I should have seen it as I observed students repeatedly listening to the same song, playing the same game, rereading the same picture book, telling the same story or the same joke, or drawing the same picture again and again.

I should have noticed it years before when my son, Ben, who was very young at the time, wanted me to read the same picture book again and again and *again*. By the time *Road Roller Saves the Day* by Jill Barnes was due back at the library, I had it entirely memorized. I should have noticed it on our next library trip when, after scouring hundreds of book spines in the children's section, he finally walked over to me wearing a great smile and holding *Road Roller Saves the Day.*

Caveat: What the Teacher Knows Isn't as Important as What the Students Already Know

I used to believe that the teacher's knowledge was one of the most important learning factors in the classroom. Certainly, the teacher's expertise is valuable, helpful, and can contribute enormously to the lesson. Yet it can also get in the way. In fact, I now believe that what the teacher already knows is one of the *least* important factors in the student's learning.

Unfortunately, teachers often build lessons based on what they already know. I've done it hundreds, if not thousands, of times. Relying on our personal knowledge is comforting, as if we're building on familiar, solid ground. But drawing on *your* knowledge is far less useful for your students than constructing a lesson that causes them to reach for and build on what *they* know. Clearly, this paradigm challenges teachers from the first moment of lesson planning.

I have come to recognize two specific personal planning methods that have had a substantial impact on the quality of my lessons. In the first method, I read an objective, or look at a lesson, and decide I already have enough background knowledge to sufficiently teach the lesson. Although it may sound ideal, I have learned that this method can actually be the most precarious option for my students. It took me many years to realize that when I plan and teach lessons from the vantage point of feeling as if I have sufficient background knowledge, the lessons almost invariably veer in the direction of my thinking. My unintentional goal becomes guiding my students to learn what I already know. Aside from focusing on my own thinking rather than helping students to reach for their own thinking, this method ends up devaluing a lifetime of learning by attempting to compress and summarize everything I know on the subject into a short block of time.

Even if a tried-and-true lesson that I thoroughly thought out in the past *could* work well with my current students, using it as-is—without updating my anticipation of student thinking—limits the learning experience. But if I revisit my lessons and take into consideration my current students' thinking, then those lessons can be very effective. However, it is important for me to think carefully about why my tried-and-true lessons actually worked in the first place. Was it because of the nature of the lesson itself? Or was it because of the anticipation the teacher carried into that specific learning community? Most likely, it was largely attached to the teacher's anticipation, which leads to another question: What exactly was the teacher anticipating? Likely, it was the effect on student thinking, and how the students—**the ones who were in the classroom when the lesson was originally developed**—were about to connect upcoming thinking to what they already knew.

The other lesson-preparation scenario occurs when I begin with anticipation for a lesson and recognize that my learning about the content is either insufficient, can be deepened, or is solid enough that I have the confidence to largely set aside my own thinking and allow substantial space for students to create their own learning. This scenario requires me to embrace a personal triumvirate: the readiness to learn, the anticipation of student thinking, and the willingness to move my thinking out of the way so students can reach for their own thinking. I've learned that good preparation is much more about "lesson anticipation" than "lesson planning." The substantial difference between "lesson planning" and "lesson anticipation" is that *planning* focuses on what I plan to happen. Lesson anticipation focuses on the unexpected and opens the door to new learning possibilities—for my students and for me.

Early in my teaching career, I based my lesson planning and teaching on my own experiences. After all, I had overcome significant challenges and navigated many experiences to understand the material. But I've ultimately come to realize that the more I insert myself into the learning experience, the more the lesson veers toward what I know. Reread that last sentence and notice whose thinking is central when my knowledge leads the way. It was not my students' thinking I focused on with that planning method; it was my own. In order to help my students reach for the value of what they already know—and to build on it—I often have to push myself out of the way.

Within the artistry of teaching lies attention to many critical decision-making moments, which are not always easy to anticipate. One of those moments has to do with knowing just when to help students to reach for their own thinking. One way you can encourage students to develop their thinking is to harness the power of writing. Writing provides an enormously powerful opportunity for students to simultaneously revisit what they have learned in the past and use it to make

> Lesson anticipation focuses on the unexpected and opens the door to new learning possibilities—for my students and for me.

sense of new information. Picture the student who is processing new learning, reaching toward existing knowledge, and is in the habit of reaching for a writing tool with plenty of space to process. That student will reach right past my thinking, and that is exactly what I want.

I am learning to move out of the way. I am learning to allow the students to reach for what they do not know by reaching for what they already know. And I suspect that, right now as you are reading this, you are attaching Big Idea 11 to your personal context, your classroom and experiences. You are reaching right past my thinking. After all, one of the most important factors in learning is what you already know.

KEY QUESTIONS

1. Why is it easier for educators to focus on what students do not yet know?

2. What are the benefits of helping students to reach for what they already know?

3. How can we provide opportunities for students to reach past our thinking?

4. Which concepts from this chapter may be both counter-intuitive and productive?

CHAPTER 12
FACING THE IMPOSSIBLE

The new. The difficult. The challenging. The seemingly impossible. That is the kind of risky territory where we constantly travel as learners.

We frequently face two options when we lead our students into highly challenging content. We can soften the challenge so that it becomes more attainable. Or we can embrace the fact that the educational territory where we are asking our students to travel is demanding—it may even *seem* impossible to navigate. Which of those two courses of action are your students most likely to thank you later for providing? Your students will thank you for allowing them to face the kinds of challenges that truly allow them to learn.

Here is the reality: If you face something and find that you struggle, that does not mean that you can't do it. Instead, it means that you are perfectly positioned for powerful learning.

So I choose to ask my students to face what seems impossible.

----------- BIG IDEA 12 -----------
WHAT SEEMS IMPOSSIBLE NOW
MAY SOON BE POSSIBLE.

Introducing the Big Idea

"Girls and boys, I have a new Big Idea to share with you today: What Seems Impossible Now May Soon Be Possible. This idea is very important because it gives us permission to do two things. First, it allows us to face really challenging ideas. Second, it gives us permission to time travel, to anticipate what the challenge may look like from the future, after we have found a way to succeed.

"Notice that it says, 'seems impossible.' The feeling that something seems impossible is an important feeling. We all experience that feeling many times. Many times life is difficult, it's challenging, and it hands us things that we feel like we can never overcome. Those times make it difficult to see past that moment.

"That is exactly where this idea invites us to time travel. It invites us to know that there are solutions, pathways, and answers. And at some point, if we choose to work hard, we can look back and realize that there was a moment that once seemed impossible, but we found a way to the possible.

If you face something and find that you struggle ... it means that you are perfectly positioned for powerful learning.

"That's a pretty amazing realization, and it's even more amazing if we anticipate it in the middle of the impossible. If something seems impossible, I want you to do the opposite of letting it stop you. I want you to notice that it is challenging, and know that there is a time—coming soon—when it will become something you are able to do.

"You can overcome what seems impossible. And you will.

"So when we step into ideas in our class that feel like they are very challenging, I want you to welcome those ideas, and I want you to remember that you will look back on the moment of difficulty and recognize that you overcame it."

The Power of Journaling

Without space to process new ideas, a student's self-perception as a learner can become impacted, especially when overcoming the "impossible" feels out of reach. Providing space to process learning before transitioning into a new subject or additional concepts honors the depth of the learning that we are asking students to explore. Journaling is an excellent way to encourage students to validate their own learning and firmly establish new layers of ideas, experiences, and connections. Allowing students time to journal in class provides them with the space to further explore challenging ideas and to begin building their thinking in personalized and powerful ways.

Journals come in a variety of styles and formats. For instance, you could provide each student with a "What Seems Impossible" journal, where they can record and review their series of successes over time. However, I think a much more practical and open-ended option is to give students a generic journal and begin giving them a variety of reflective icons to use in it. For example, you could ask the students to jot a symbol that represents "seems impossible" next to a journal entry. It will be helpful to you, as a reader of the journal, to teach the class a single, shared icon. An icon to represent what seems impossible may simply be a stop sign with the word "seems" above it.

Other types of icons you may want to share with your students could include the following:

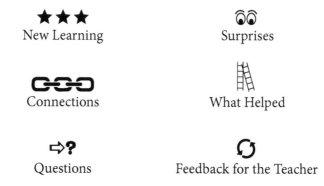

When I was student teaching, my mentor teacher, John Emerson, introduced me to student academic journals. One of the most practical tips he shared with me in terms of managing these journals was to use five different colors of journals (or to somehow code the journals) so that one journal color would be collected on Mondays, another color on Tuesdays, and so on. That single tip allowed me to sustain the process of interacting with student journals because I soon learned that I could not keep up with reading all reflections every day. Eventually, I moved to four categories of journals rather than five, because I was often exhausted on Friday. It also helped me to keep pace on four-day weeks.

Another tip for implementing student journaling is to encourage students to only write on the top half of each page. The blank space on the bottom of the page is not for teacher responses. If you choose to use responses, try to keep your responses in the margins of the journal. The white space on the bottom of the page may seem like a waste of paper initially. However, that space is for students to eventually go back and interact with their earlier thinking. At some point, a student may return to that stop sign with the word "seems" above it, read what is written next to that stop sign, and recognize and journal in the white space below that entry about something that seemed impossible and has become possible—even easy. Imagine the effect that kind of self-affirmation could have on the student the next time he or she sketches a stop sign with the word "seems" above it. That stop sign may even become a welcome icon for a student who now understands in a personal way that facing what seems difficult can yield impressive growth. That student may begin to anticipate and seek out the types of connections that lead into the heart of what seems impossible.

I strongly encourage you to not limit student journaling opportunities to the end of the class. Invite students to reflect throughout the class and to write in their journals at any point during the lesson. Not all students will take you up on this, especially when you first suggest it. But there may come a time when, in the middle of a lesson, you notice a student opening a journal and jotting down a question. Or you might look around and see several students responding to your instruction, or their interactions, with surprises, sketches, and other notes that reflect their processing, thinking, and wondering right in the midst of the lesson. These students are not off-task. They are possibly more on-task than you had even hoped. In those moments, you will know that your students are making connections by revealing their thinking to themselves, and to you as well. And remember, learning is about making connections.

How the Idea Grew

Much like my students, I am encouraged by the idea of "time travel" in terms of challenges. Looking back through my journaling allows me to see what I have already overcome. But there is value in projecting forward as well. Looking at a challenge from the perspective of knowing that I will be able to look back on it to see what I learned because of it encourages me to push ahead. When I see a challenge, I try to also look beyond the challenge to the victory on the other side.

As a teacher, Big Idea 12 challenged me—and gave me permission—to lead my students into difficult territory. The idea prompts me to ask tough questions—questions that cannot always be answered in a day, a week, or even in a month. I realized that many of the questions that are most worth asking are the ones that cannot be easily answered. This Big Ideas invites me to ask my students to do things that feel like they are out of reach.

Perhaps best of all, Big Idea 12 reminds me that I need not place artificial, protective boundaries on myself or my students. We understand that learning challenges will arise. We also understand that if we work hard, we can overcome those challenges and look back on our accomplishments with pride. No, I do not soften the challenge. My students and I expectantly dare to venture into new and risky learning territory. We know that what seems impossible now may soon be possible. But in order for that to happen, we have to be willing to face the impossible.

KEY QUESTIONS

1. How do your students respond to what seems impossible?

2. Do you feel free to present "impossible" challenges to your students?

3. How can you leverage the power of journaling in your classroom?

4. Would you be willing to accept a professional challenge that you initially had no idea how to accomplish, such as starting a blog, presenting at a conference, writing a book, or impacting students and educators around the world?

5. Can you think of some other examples of professional growth opportunities that seem ridiculously out of reach, yet you know you would grow from them?

6. What is stopping you from deciding to embrace the "impossible?"

CHAPTER 13
FACING THE POSSIBLE

Although some students are still wary of making mistakes, I've learned there is something that makes some students, and adults, even more nervous: finding their best. They are afraid to discover what their best is—what they're truly capable of doing.

Big Idea 13 lands squarely in classrooms where we often ask students to "do their best."

BIG IDEA 13
YOU CANNOT KNOW WHAT YOUR BEST IS IF YOU DO NOT TRY TO APPROACH IT.

Introducing the Big Idea

"Girls and boys, today I have a new Big Idea to share with you, and it is powerful! Big Idea 13 is this: "You Cannot Know What Your Best Is if You Do Not Try to Approach It."

"I want to tell you something that might surprise you. Some people are afraid of finding out what their best is. They are afraid that they will discover that their best is not as good as they had hoped. So instead of finding out what it is, they shy away from it.

"For some people, reaching for their best is empowering. But for other people, the idea of finding out what their best is feels like it places limits on them. They are afraid that when they find their best, they will find the end of their growth.

"I want to tell you something new—and I want to be very clear—you will never find the end of your growth."

I turn around and draw a horizontal line on the board. Next to the line I write, "Your Best."

"This line that says "Your Best" is not something that stays in one place in your life. It grows and changes and moves as you continue to learn. As you learn, as you improve, as you face challenges and move past what used to seem impossible, this line moves."

I erase the line and draw it noticeably higher on the board.

"Your best improves as you learn. Just as important, what you've learned impacts what you are able to learn next."

"As you keep facing the impossible, as you keep trying, learning, stumbling, and succeeding, you will continue to approach this line. And it will keep moving."

Again, I erase the line and draw it noticeably higher on the board.

"I am not nearly as interested in what your best is right now as I am in seeing you try to approach it because I know you will find out that your best will continue to grow as you chase it. Take a risk, take a chance, go after it and see what happens."

I turn to look at the board, erase the line again, and then stand on a chair and "redraw" it by sticking masking tape as far above the board as I can reach.

"Don't be afraid that you will find your limits. But do pay attention to this: You cannot know what your best is if you do not try to approach it. I am excited to watch you chase your best! And I'm excited to see what happens when you do!"

How the Idea Grew

Big Idea 13 is a powerful concept for my students. It also applies to me and my own growth. I cannot know what my best is, as an educator, if I do not try to approach it. For this reason, I am compelled to reach for growth, to surround myself with those who are hungry to grow, and to understand that when I am satisfied, I certainly have not found my best. And while I fully recognize I do not have time to rapidly improve every area of my practice, I can choose areas to intentionally pursue.

This idea took root for me personally in another way as well. While I had long believed in the value of improving in my areas of weakness, through this Big Idea, I came to appreciate the importance of focusing on and improving in my areas of strength. Doing so unleashes the incredible potential to develop true expertise that can be shared with others. As you grow your strengths and reflect upon them, and especially as you share them with others, take note of what happens to the "weaknesses" that you chose not to place your focus on. Notice what happens to your confidence. Then, notice what happens to your "best." I suspect you'll discover that you will redefine your "best" every time you authentically stretch for it.

You cannot know what your best is if you do not try to approach it!

Key Questions

1. Have you ever shared this idea with your students?

2. In what ways have you risked pursuing your best?

3. Which of these is scarier to you: Presenting at a major conference two years from now, or not spending those two years stretching to become your best?

CHAPTER 14
The Most Important
Big Idea

One of the most important questions you can ask yourself as an educator is this: What do you truly believe about students? What do you believe about their potential?

This is exactly the question that landed in front of me during a college class well before I ever became a teacher. "What do you believe about students?" I was given a few days to ponder the question and express my thoughts in a short essay. Although I had very little experience working with students at that point, I managed to complete the essay and arrive at the statement: "I believe that all students can learn."

If you think about it, that's a very weak statement for an educator to make. Of course, all students can learn! That is an obvious truth, and furthermore it takes no risks. It does not dare to approach the potential students possess, and it does not delve into any deeper questions.

To be fair, my very limited experience of working directly with students had not given me a chance to really understand their potential. I had not been amazed by their creativity. I had not walked out of a lesson absolutely inspired by what my students had just achieved. I had not had the opportunity to be stunned by their enormous adaptability, shocked by their insights, or overwhelmed by their potential.

When I stepped into my teaching career, my students astounded me. They gifted me with many changes in perspective and caused me to rethink my answer to that essay question.

What do I believe about students now?

Students are absolutely amazing! They possess a stunning, remarkable, absolutely awe-inspiring potential that has no boundaries. I am deeply in awe of every single one of them. Every day that I am in the presence of students, I am deeply inspired.

Today, I appreciate the truth that a statement as small as "I believe all students can learn," limits students. Students are stunningly bright, capable, creative, and purely amazing. Of course they can learn. A better question is "How well are we matching our students' potential with the learning opportunities that we are providing in class?" How are we reconciling that potential in light of the fact that we have a group of amazing learners gathered together in a classroom community? Are those students interacting, producing ideas, and learning from one another? Or instead, are we limiting them with our idea of a lesson's intended outcome?

The beliefs we hold about our students will deeply impact us personally and professionally. They will also profoundly impact our students. It is impossible to hide our beliefs about our students, especially from our students themselves. What we truly believe about them shines through all of our interactions, our body language, our tone of voice, our assignments, how we respond to students, and what we value.

Imagine two students in two different classrooms. In one classroom, although the teacher believes all students can learn, he hasn't yet dared to explore what he believes about students any further than that. In the other classroom, the teacher fully understands that every single student has a stunning capacity that should be pursued by both the teacher and the student. That teacher also clearly and constantly communicates to her students that she believes they possess remarkable potential for taking risks, expressing ideas, making connections and actively pursuing new learning. Will these students have different experiences? Absolutely!

No matter how prepared or organized the first teacher is, no matter how much effort he expends, no matter how much time he spends on preparation, he will constantly be held back by his limited belief about students. In fact, that teacher may even offer only a narrowing slice of learning to his students based on those self-imposed limitations. It quickly translates to, "I believe that students can learn about factoring ... or Westward expansion ... or genres ... or mitosis." And when not all students are successful on assignments, that belief becomes even more limited.

> ## Our beliefs about our students will deeply impact our students' beliefs in themselves.

By contrast, the teacher who has wrestled with the question, "What do you truly believe about students?" and has arrived at the realization that students are absolutely amazing will provide an entirely different learning experience.

Here is the reality: with every question, with every follow-up question, with every comment, with every response, with every lesson, and in every interaction, our beliefs about our students are evident to them. And those beliefs deeply impact our students' beliefs in themselves.

When I finally understood how absolutely amazing students are, I could not keep that profound truth to myself. It wasn't about me. It was about the students. I wanted the message to be very clear, so after I explained my beliefs and growing understandings to them, I posted the next Big Idea on the wall.

BIG IDEA 14
You Are Amazing!
Expect Much of Yourself!

I point to these words often and remind my students of what I truly believe about them and their potential. This Big Idea is the most profound epiphany of my career, and it is the concept that I want every student and educator to most deeply understand.

Introducing the Big Idea

"Today we have a new Big Idea. It says, "You Are Amazing! Expect Much of Yourself!"

"You are absolutely amazing! You are extraordinary learners. I am fortunate to be your teacher. I don't want you to walk through a single day without understanding how amazing you are. If I tried to measure how much you are able to learn, I could never do it. If I tried to describe what you could possibly do, I would never find the words. In fact, no words can come close to describing how amazing you truly are.

"Thank you for letting me learn with you. You are absolutely amazing! What an honor it is to be your teacher!

"I also want you to know something else. I want you to know how crucial it is that you realize how important you are, and that you expect a lot of yourself. I'm not describing being perfect. I'm describing how much you can grow, how you can pursue your potential, how you can learn in powerful, amazing ways. You are amazing! Expect much of yourself!"

From the day I first shared this epiphany with my students, I began referencing this Big Idea in key moments. I started thanking them for the privilege of being in their presence, and I let them know that I intended to honor their amazing potential by being the best teacher that I knew how to be.

You can likely see the profound difference this understanding of my students has made on me personally and professionally. My paradigm has shifted from something so limited to something that has deeply motivated me each time I have the privilege of walking into a classroom of amazing learners. My students know I believe that learning with them is a privilege!

Now, I don't want to communicate that everything suddenly became easier, and I certainly do not want to project that the challenges of school or classroom life suddenly disappeared, because they did not. Those challenges still exist, and I face them the best I can each day.

However, my perspective changed, and I believe my attitude and this Big Idea changed my students' perspective as well. The clarity of this understanding illuminated a sense of possibility that created a momentum that helped carry them through the challenges that are part of daily classroom life. I am convinced that there is a profound difference in the behavior and demeanor of students who are being guided by a teacher who deeply believes in them. Students reach for learning in a much different way when they see it within the context of their potential.

How the Idea Grew

Like all of the Big Ideas I am discovering on my journey as an educator, this Big Idea is layered with multiple meanings. One important message found in this Big Idea is not only directed to the students. It speaks to the teacher as well.

Read this again, from your personal vantage point: "You are amazing! Expect much of yourself!"

The role of any educator is both significant and profound. Simply by virtue of the role and our connection with students, what we all do is immensely important. Yet there is so much more.

We are all on a personal learning journey. It is a journey without boundaries, a journey that cannot be contained unless we choose to limit it ourselves. The journey is meant to be active, interactive, and lived out in our classrooms.

Although I have taught many lessons where I have felt like I have completely failed, I have also learned to not let those experiences define me. Instead, I have learned to allow those temporary failures to prompt reflection experiences and propel my personal learning journey forward.

I choose to look at the powerful message on the wall: "You Are Amazing! Expect Much of Yourself!" Truly, it is a privilege to be in a profession surrounded by fellow educators who are powerfully creative, deeply passionate, stunningly insightful, and immensely generous.

The demands of the job are high, and fatigue is often not far away. So even though this message was born out of deep recognition of each student's potential, seeing the reminder on the wall has been powerful for me as well. While I am inspired by the students, I am also inspired to remember that *I* am creative. It is invigorating to remember that I am allowed to pursue my own growth and to expect much of myself. It is perfectly fine to take risks. In fact, it is essential. I have learned that, as an educator, the quickest route to exhaustion is *not* taking risks—not pushing the boundaries of personal growth. Doing the same thing the same way again and again is one of the quickest routes to fatigue. The reason is simple: We are energized by new learning. When there are no new experiences, no risks, no adrenaline, no new stories to share, we grow bored and weary—not better.

However, when I see the Big Idea, "You Are Amazing! Expect Much of Yourself!" I am reminded that I can and *should* take growth risks. I should expect much of myself. I should try something new. I am capable of it, and I am willing to learn from it. My expectations should be high for my students. My expectations for myself should be just as high.

I challenge you to take a powerful risk. Delve deeply into your beliefs about students. Wrestle with those beliefs. Allow your daily

> **The quickest route to exhaustion is not taking risks —not pushing the boundaries of personal growth.**

interactions with students to inform those beliefs. Risk forward. Risk your very paradigms.

When you explore your capacity as an educator and as a learner, you will find the opposite of fatigue. You will find invigoration, and your students will reflect that invigoration!

Like your students, you are amazing! Expect much of yourself!

KEY QUESTIONS

1. Have you truly wrestled with the question, "What do you believe about students?" If not, how would you answer the question?

2. Have you communicated your beliefs with your students?

3. Is your personal potential shining through in the classroom?

4. Have you given yourself permission to pursue your potential?

5. If not, what is standing in your way?

6. What are some actions that you can take to pursue your own potential?

CHAPTER 15
Choosing Clarity

Powerful learners set ambitious goals and courageously pursue them. The pursuit of challenging learning can be greatly accelerated simply by providing clarity. Often, we set goals that provide us with direction and motivation. Yet taking just a moment more to add clarity to those goals by bringing definition to the process can be very beneficial. The next Big Idea provides a simple step to bring clarity to far-reaching goals.

BIG IDEA 15
The Clearer Your Goal Is, the Nearer You Are to It.

Introducing the Big Idea

"Boys and girls, this is Big Idea 15: "The Clearer Your Goal Is, the Nearer You Are to It." We set goals to reach for things we really want to attain. One of the most important parts of setting a goal is that it causes us to decide what is really important to us. We rarely set goals related to unimportant ideas. Instead, we set goals by thinking carefully about what is important. Setting a goal, such as becoming an excellent artist, a strong writer, or a helpful representative of other people, gives us a focus and a direction. However, it doesn't always give us enough direction to tell us how to reach that goal.

"So I want to introduce an important word: 'by.'"

I turn to write "BY" on the board.

"Sometimes, just by adding this word to our goal, we can actually move closer to the goal. Instead of saying, 'I want to become a great basketball player,' I can say, 'I want to become a great basketball player by...'"

I invite the students to help me complete the sentence as I start recording their responses in the form of a bulleted list:

- by learning how to dribble.
- by practicing every day.
- by making my shots.
- by making my free throws.
- by learning the rules.
- by catching the ball.
- by knowing where I am on the court.
- by watching great players.
- by learning from the referees.
- by teaching others how to play.
- by making three-point shots.

- by getting the ball.

- by stealing the ball.

- by listening to my coach.

- by playing games.

"I think this list could go on and on—just like your learning can go on and on. I don't know everything that we could write on this list, but I do know that the goal just became clearer, so you are closer to it.

"If your goal is to become a great basketball player, then you have a starting point. But a much more helpful way to think about it may be, 'I want to become a great basketball player by learning the rules, by practicing every day, and by playing in games.' The clearer your goal is, the nearer you are to it.

"Your goal may become clearer, and you may move closer to accomplishing it, just by wondering what follows the word 'by.' The clearer your goal is, the nearer you are to accomplishing it."

When students are determined to continually grow, they almost always benefit from highly specific feedback coupled with a growing understanding of how to respond to that feedback. They also benefit from being able to see clear steps toward their goals. Simply using the word "by" may help them identify those steps.

How the Idea Grew

Some of the places where my risks have turned into unfortunate stumbles in the classroom have been the same places where, upon reflection, I realized that my goals were actually vague aims and, as such, did not have clear targets to pull me forward.

For example, I wanted a classroom culture that valued thinking and where students propelled their learning through the free exchange of ideas. When this did not happen, I was not sure where to look. I did not even know what questions to ask or how to effectively reflect upon the experience. Eventually, I realized I had not deeply considered the specific steps I needed to take in order to reach that goal.

In contrast, when I became more specific, saying, for example, "I want my students to exchange observations by using the stem, 'I Notice ...'" I observed that I could reflect about the success of the strategy rather than whether or not I had met my goal, which in reality was probably several steps away.

Attaching the word "by" to a desired outcome lets me set bigger, riskier goals. Identifying the steps to my goal means that I do not have to wrap my mind around the entire goal all at once. As discussed with Big Idea 12, I knew that what seems impossible can soon become possible, especially if I provide myself with the kind of clarity that helps me to move forward. Rather than feeling overwhelmed, I can instead focus on each "by" as I work my way through the unknown and closer to attaining the goal.

After resetting my goals with clear steps, I determined that, upon reaching my goal, I would take time to reflect. I would acknowledge the success and learn from it. After all, there is much learning in front of me, and I want to learn all I can from both my failures and my successes.

Attaching the word "by" to a desired outcome lets me set bigger, riskier goals.

KEY QUESTIONS

1. How often do you take the risk of setting goals that you have no idea how to attain?

2. What is one goal that you would like to achieve that seems to be entirely out of reach at the moment?

3. How would using "by" bring clarity to you or your students?

4. How does using "by" move a goal that feels lofty and out of reach from the seemingly impossible toward the possible?

5. To which other Big Ideas does this connect?

CHAPTER 16
THE RESOURCE WE
CANNOT RECYCLE

Regardless of our status, or where we live, or how our individual lives compare to anyone else's, we all share one reality equally: time.

Time is a resource that we cannot recycle.

I am not talking about time zones, daylight savings, or any nuances of representations of time. I am talking about moments and what we choose to do with them. Like this moment, right now. More specifically, I am talking about our moments in the classroom.

Time in the classroom is precious. It is limited. And what we choose to do with that time is important.

Your time is precious. The time of each student in every classroom is precious. How we choose to use our time and how we choose to value one another's time is deeply important. Furthermore, the way we choose to use the students' time speaks loudly about our belief in them and has the potential to deeply impact our relationships with our students.

BIG IDEA 16
TIME IS PRECIOUS.

Introducing the Big Idea

"Girls and boys, today I'm going to introduce a new Big Idea. It says, 'Time Is Precious.' We only have one chance to live today. What we do with today is important. What we do with each moment is important. This Big Idea will be on the wall tomorrow, but when you read it tomorrow you will know that today has gone. We can look back and wonder, 'What did we do with our day?' 'What risks did we take?' 'What were the experiences that we can continue to learn from?'

"You also need to know that time is precious to every other person in this class, and you are contributing to his or her experience today. As a classroom community, we have a responsibility to one another to make the most of our time together.

"Time is precious!"

How the Idea Grew

Please make no assumption that I make the best use of all my time. My wife, Jeannine, would likely laugh at that thought, since she is the one who most often sees me experiencing the deep importance of "down time" in the hours and seasons when I am exhausted from my efforts at school.

But when I see this statement in the classroom, I am reminded that classroom time is extremely precious and that it needs to be approached thoughtfully and strategically.

Students have only so much time during the school day, so I need to maximize their opportunities to learn, to think, and to grow. One way I can do that is by talking less so the students can think more.

> ## Very often, I need to talk less so the students can think more.

I periodically pause to count the voices in the classroom. If I can't count past one, I know I need to rethink what I am doing with the time. I need to ask practical questions like these:

Am I asking students to write during the lesson?

What kinds of individual thinking actions am I requiring of the students?

What kinds of interpersonal thinking opportunities am I including?

Am I providing students opportunities to share their thinking with one another?

When students share their thinking, are they spending too much time trying to interpret how I am hoping they will work together, or are they moving directly into the thinking?

Is this lesson experience worthy of each one of the student's time?

Is it worthy of my time?

Is this lesson so important that we will refer to it later?

The Edges of the Day

Another way to make the most of the precious time in the classroom is to use the "edges of the day." The very beginning of the day, the very end of the day, and all of the transitional moments throughout the day provide unique and valuable relational opportunities.

In elementary schools, the edges of the day may include the first part of the morning and the end of the day. In secondary schools, the edges of the periods often offer powerful opportunities to interact with students and to meaningfully and personally build connections and develop relationships.

Here are a few things you have potential to communicate during the edges of the day:

"Good morning."

"Welcome to school."

"I am truly glad that you are here today."

"I hope you have a great day!"

"You are an amazing learner, and I can't wait to see what you do today!"

"How are you?"

Now reread each one of those statements again, this time picturing your students saying them to you.

In addition to the edges of your day or class periods, you can also deliberately seize wedges of time, right in the middle of the day. Those transitional moments, which may only be a few seconds long, afford clear opportunities to express important messages to students. These moments of time, the edges and wedges of the day, offer you powerful

> The edges of the day offer powerful opportunities to personally and meaningfully connect with your students.

opportunities to personally and meaningfully connect with your students. They help you build relationships, detect personalization opportunities, convey your beliefs about students, and set the tone of your choosing.

How do these important edges of the day relate to the rest of the day? They shape the way your students will spend their day or class period. When you make an intentional decision to connect with and communicate belief, positivity, energy, and enthusiasm to your students, you set or reset the tone the students will experience for the rest of the day. It only takes students a moment to detect the level of your passion and focus. Many times, they will perceive your mood and your commitment to them at the first edge of the day, right when they walk into your classroom. What will they detect in that moment?

KEY QUESTIONS

1. In your schedule, where are the "edges" of your day?

2. How can you leverage the power of the "edges of the day?"

3. This chapter included several examples of what the first "edge of the day" might sound like. What is missing from the list?

4. What types of powerful statements might you hear at the end of the day?

5. What are some strategies you can use to maximize the amount of time available for student thinking?

6. What is one action you can take to make a lesson extremely powerful and memorable for students?

7. When you take additional steps to make a lesson extraordinary, what messages does that send to the students?

8. How might your use of classroom time impact your relationships with your students?

CHAPTER 17
DEEPER, RICHER, AND STRONGER, INSTEAD OF MORE

Learning is about making connections. This is an idea that grew in many different ways over time. Before this statement pointed to the power of relationships within the classroom community, it presented the idea that we connect new learning to existing learning.

There is a great deal of power in examining current learning and current understandings. Many times, powerful learning opportunities emerge when we shift our focus from learning "new ideas" to learning more about what we already know—or at least what we have begun to understand.

Ideas can be grown. They can be developed. They can be examined and furthered. This is a clear reality that rubs against the grain of our need for completion and tidiness in learning. If there is one word that fails to describe learning, it is "tidy."

Consider how messy, and amazing, and beautiful, and complicated learning is in a classroom setting where so many unique students are learning and growing their ideas about the same concept using several different methods. Understandings may constantly be developing, sprouting, extending, and connecting in a wide variety of ways that we were neither intending nor anticipating.

A tempting inclination to respond to the messiness of classroom learning may be to attempt to contain it to the measurable, to the succinct, to the quantifiable. Don't do it. Instead, acknowledge that learning is a natural and often untamed expression of how we make sense of our encounters with life. And frequently, life is messy.

It is true that those specific, identifiable parts of content learning are extremely important.

Yet there is much more that can be unleashed if we resist the urge to contain learning to activities and outcomes that can be easily identified or measured.

There is the wild dare into the very nature of learning that can feel extremely risky. It is a risk into the unknown and the unpredictable. It can be very uncomfortable. But that is the very risk that needs to be embraced. So I posted the next Big Idea on the wall.

BIG IDEA 17
Grow Your Ideas.

Introducing the Big Idea

"Today I would like to share a new Big Idea. This is Big Idea 17: 'Grow Your Ideas.' You are powerful learners with powerful ideas. The ideas that you have will become bigger and deeper and stronger as you learn more about them.

"You can use those ideas to help you understand new ideas. But you can do something else, too. You can use the ideas that you have to help you understand your own ideas more and more.

"When you learn something new, that is not the end of your learning about that idea. Learning something new is a beginning. It is the start of a journey with that idea. Your learning will grow and grow and grow. I want you to understand that learning does not come in completed packages. Learning grows.

"When you learn something new, it may feel powerful and amazing. Because it is. But it is also a beginning. It opens up the door to learning even more. It is important to understand that new learning is not an end. New learning is a beginning, especially when we decide to grow that learning. Especially when we decide to grow our ideas.

"Let your learning become big. Give it space to grow. Expect to learn more and more about what you are learning. Don't wait for someone else to help your ideas to grow. You be the one to make your ideas grow. You be the one to cause your learning to become rich, and deep, and strong. You be the one to grow your ideas.

"That is exactly what our new Big Idea means. It says, 'Grow Your Ideas.' As we learn together, let's all do that. Let's all grow our ideas!"

How the Idea Grew

This Big Idea creates space for students and teachers to seek a growing depth of understanding over time. I have discovered that it provides an unexpected freedom to me as a teacher. This concept allowed me to pursue a further understanding that the depth and richness of learning does not have to be contained within a single lesson.

Growing our ideas means that we are never finished with them. In fact, it signifies the opposite. If these ideas are truly important, we will certainly return to them. Sometimes we return to them in ways that are anticipated or carefully orchestrated. Yet due to the wild nature of learning, we may return to ideas unexpectedly. When that happens, we may be surprised by unplanned, but welcomed, growth.

KEY QUESTIONS

1. In what ways is learning wild, messy, and untamed?

2. Why is there a temptation to try to contain learning?

3. How can the concept of "Grow Your Ideas" empower your students?

4. How can it empower you?

5. What does "a wild dare into the very nature of learning" mean to you?

6. In what way is learning risky? Why is that important?

CHAPTER 18
A TREASURE WORTH
DISCOVERING

Early on, I thought answers were of great importance. I believed the point of learning was to find the answers, to know how to find the answers, and to settle the questions.

I felt that questions deserved answers and that answers settled questions. That meant the questions I allowed to linger the longest were the ones that I knew could eventually be brought to completion. Sometimes that required waiting for the answers.

Waiting is seldom easy, but it is often very important. Wait time provides students necessary space to process toward an answer, and I found it to be highly effective at causing me to delay my interruptions of student thinking. I learned how to wait … and then to wait a little longer … and then to wait beyond my point of discomfort. This effective technique helped my students understand that I had little intention of being the one to provide the answer to the question.

Wait time, however, held a greater power than I initially detected.

What I did not realize was that answers were not the most important responses. Even though, early in my career, I used questions to seek answers, I eventually realized that questions could uncover something far more important than simply answers. A well-placed question could cause students to think of important questions of their own—questions that lead to wonder, investigation, and discovery. So I began using questions to seek something much more valuable than answers: I was seeking other questions.

Some of my lessons began with simple questions that led to simple answers. "What is one-third of fifteen?" was met with manipulatives scraping across desktops and students pointing to piles, or stacks, or groups. Some students moved together, shoved most of the cubes aside and then counted out fifteen in front of them. More sliding, more scraping, and more conversation ensued. Eventually some groups arrived at formations resembling three groups of five and continued discussing from that point. Other students set blocks on paper and sketched circles around groups of five, clearly showing three circles, three groups of five. The discussion turned to the number five. One-third of fifteen is five, and there was photo-worthy evidence on the desks and in the sketches to back the answer.

Yes, the discussion proved powerful, and the evidence was abundant. But it was not what I wanted my students to discover. It was merely an answer. A single answer to a small question.

Because I feel little reward, as a teacher, when a single question is polished off with a single answer, I look for the rougher edges that are more difficult to polish. Those edges are the ones that often yield the greatest rewards.

So I pressed on. "What is two-thirds of fifteen?" With mixed reactions, students examined their desks. Some reviewed their three evenly distributed piles of fifteen. Others, to my great surprise, completely dismantled their arrangements and started from scratch. A few of them looked at me carefully, wondering about the connection to the previous question. One by one, the groups arrived at the conclusion that two-thirds of fifteen was ten. Another answer polished off.

So I pressed on. "What is three-thirds of fifteen?" This question produced answers more quickly, partially because the students detected a useful pattern. After all, one of the many connections we found useful in this case was that every third of fifteen was equal to five. So two-thirds of fifteen was equal to two fives, and three-thirds of fifteen was equal to three fives. It was another answer, and it was useful, but it was not a satisfying conclusion. It was not what I was seeking. It was not what I was waiting for. But that moment was coming.

"Great! What is four-thirds of fifteen?"

And then I waited, and listened.

"It's twenty because every third is equal to five. So four of them is equal to twenty."

Another student, without waiting for me, inserted "No, you can't have four-thirds of fifteen. You can only have three-thirds of fifteen. There are only fifteen. You can't have more."

Another student responded, "But each third is five, so four thirds would be twenty."

An awkward pause. My opportunity to provide a rescue. Of course, sometimes the best rescue for a point of dissonance is to leave it unanswered, to continue to let the dissonance ring loudly.

As an aside, let me address the moment of rescue. You may face this anxious moment often. When students do not know an answer, feel unsure, or need help to reach an answer or a point of understanding, that is the moment when your most powerful inclination may be to step in and provide the answer, or nudge them in exactly the right direction with a single helpful fact.

Here is what to do in that moment: wait. Just wait. Do not insert yourself between the students and the opportunity to face dissonance and challenge. This is the exact point to test your mettle with wait time. This is the point where the students may just discover something much more important and far more powerful than an answer. They may discover a question! Recognize the moment, and put your wait-time mettle to the test. This may be precisely the moment when students begin generating the most important questions. That is a powerful and important experience. Allow it to unfold.

"I think the answer is zero! You can't have four-thirds of fifteen. It's not possible. So it's zero. Look there are only fifteen. You can't have more than fifteen. So it's zero."

"Well, I notice that every third is five more than the one before. So this must be 5 more."

"I agree. That's a great notice. But look. There are only fifteen cubes. There can't be more than fifteen. Fifteen is the most. So I think the answer is fifteen."

Mentally noting that the conversation has become owned, I observe, and I wait for it. And finally it begins to develop.

"Mr. Wyborney, is it even possible to have four-thirds of fifteen?"

Wait for it. The question is on its way.

"Hmmm…" I wonder aloud. "What is fifteen?"

"It's the blocks. There are fifteen."

"There are fifteen blocks," I echo. "Can you give me four-thirds of them?"

The resulting murmur eventually returns a "No, not unless you give some back."

"Wait," I hear from another desk, previously very quiet. "I have five more blocks. You can have three-thirds from that desk, and five more from me…" a slight hesitation. "But that would be twenty. Never mind."

An answer. An incomplete answer—the kind of answer that is leaning toward an important question. A perfect opportunity. And clearly this is not the place for wait time. A wrong answer—one that the student self-detected as either incorrect or incomplete but was not sure why. It is a self-detection that is resting on something powerful, something that could easily be brushed aside by the momentum of the conversation. So I simply insert, "Hmmm… why wouldn't the extra blocks work?"

The previously quiet student sits up a little straighter, and still in the process of thinking it through begins to add, "Well, that would take twenty blocks and there are only fifteen. To give you four-thirds we would have to give you twenty, but there aren't twenty. There are only fifteen. We would have to change the number to twenty. But then it wouldn't be four-thirds of fifteen." She pauses, but she is not finished. "The real question is can you even have an improper fraction of another number?"

And there it is!

And now the lesson is positioned to win.

We have discovered a question. It is the kind of question that will lead to more questions.

That is the moment I have been waiting for, and I am going to point it toward further clarity.

I'm kinetic now! "Is it possible to have an improper fraction of another number? Let's write that down! I wonder how many different ways we can state that question?"

In this moment, I know that I could have rapidly taught the students how to calculate seven-thirds of twenty-four. It would only have taken a few minutes of our precious time. They would have arrived at fifty-six. Or ten-thirds of thirty-nine. It's 130. But all we would have discovered would have been products, and I am not sure they could really even be called discoveries. That process would have been successful but would not have valued our time with worthwhile learning.

Instead, I waited for the question. We were in pursuit of questions, not answers, and we had now nearly arrived at a rich one.

When wait time leads to an answer it is useful. When it leads to a question, it is extraordinary.

Some students looked at the blocks, some looked at the quickly scribbled question on the board, and some had their eyes on me. And I was pointing to Big Idea 18.

"Excellent! You have just discovered a question. What other questions can it lead us to?"

"Is it possible to give someone an improper fraction of a whole number? If it is, can you give me some examples of when that might be true?"

"In fact, can we go a step further? Can we identify examples of certain kinds of situations in which it is possible to consider an improper fraction of a whole number—and other situations in which it is not possible? Then we can sort those situations. We can compare and contrast those situations to see what we learn. Why are they sometimes separate, when do they overlap, and most importantly…"

I know we have finally reached the question now.

"Most importantly, what does this question teach us about how math describes our lives?"

--- **BIG IDEA 18** ---

DISCOVER A QUESTION.

Introducing the Big Idea

"We know that there may be many pathways to a correct answer. We also know that there may be many correct answers. However, we haven't explored the quality of the questions that launch us on those journeys. There are many different kinds of questions. Some questions are fairly simple and can be answered without much time or thought. Other questions are more powerful—much more powerful. Those questions cause us to think and to wonder deeply. Sometimes those questions are so powerful that they lead us to many other important questions.

"When we find powerful questions, we also find opportunities to look for multiple pathways. Powerful questions have the potential to set us on powerful journeys.

"You are extraordinary, amazing, and powerful learners. Your potential is enormous, staggering, and beyond anything that I can ever imagine. As you learn, I want you to focus on one more layer. I want you to start looking for questions that are powerful. Don't just look for answers or pathways. Also look for questions. Look for important questions. Look for the kinds of questions that cause us all to think deeply. I want us to be discoverers of questions.

"This is Big Idea 18: 'Discover a Question.'"

If you are waiting to find out how I wrapped up the lesson, I have to point out that my job as a teacher is not to wrap up questions. My job is to unwrap questions.

I could have chosen, for the sake of efficiency of time, to provide several examples where it is and is not possible to have four-thirds of fifteen.

I could have said that if your complete set consists of fifteen—a universal set of fifteen— you cannot hand someone four-thirds of the fifteen objects from that set.

> **My job as a teacher is not to wrap up questions. My job is to unwrap questions.**

Likewise, I could have said that fifteen only sometimes represents an ultimate quantity. If one-third of an expected group of fifteen arrived at a party, and more kept trickling in until there were four-thirds of the expected fifteen guests, we would realize that fifteen may represent a portion of a much bigger possibility.

Sometimes, we pay four-thirds of the fifteen dollars we budgeted.

Sometimes, we spend four-thirds of the fifteen minutes we had planned to finish a project.

Sometimes, we drink four-thirds of a 15 oz. beverage thanks to refills, and we may even wonder how many ounces we just consumed.

I mentioned none of this. Instead, I posted the question on the board and let it linger. I allowed us to wonder. And this was the better use of wait time.

"Is it possible to give someone an improper fraction of a whole number?"

"What does this question teach us about how math describes our lives?"

How the Idea Grew

Did you notice the shift that took place at the moment the first question was discovered? Many moments of opportunity overlap in our lessons. The decision about which opportunity to pursue depends largely on your understanding of your students.

Overlapping opportunity moments include the transfer of ownership, the launch of wondering, the extension of prior understanding, the movement toward a question, and the arrival at a question. All of these occurrences can overlap, so it is easy to overlook one of the most important shifts of all, which is the one that happened at nearly the same moment the question was discovered.

The lesson shifted. It shifted from calculation to wondering about real-life context. And in that moment, the lesson moved from partially interesting to very important.

Discovering questions not only propels a lesson forward, it points the wondering of the lesson toward the important.

I want my students to ask:

- What can I do with this?

- How does this make me more powerful?

- What are the opportunities or circumstances that are happening in my life right now that this applies to?

- What do I see clearly now that I didn't even notice before?

I want my students to say, "Now I can look for those connections. The things that I am learning in class are all about my life and what is happening right now around me. I am going to search for the connections to my life, and I am going to find them. I am out to discover a question, and that is what this lesson is about. It is not about the objective on the board. It is about finding out how this is connected to my life. I am becoming a questioner. I am becoming someone who searches for questions, finds questions, and seeks to find meaning in those questions."

As for me, I realize that I am discovering a bigger, broader, more important objective than any content objective that is on the front white board. The greater objective is the one on my wall that says, "Discover a Question," because *that* objective invites students to reach for the personal context of the content that we are discovering.

Obviously, answers have an important place in education. What can be less obvious is the necessity of seeking and discovering new questions. The ability to generate meaningful questions is a powerful asset for all learners. Yet waiting for important questions can make us uncomfortable. Reaching those questions often requires an entirely different level of wait time. So it may often be necessary to outwait our discomfort to get to the most meaningful questions.

The risk I choose to embrace is to encourage my students to discover questions. I step into the lesson looking for a question to be discovered, and when it appears, I capture it. I am entirely certain I will miss the important questions if I am only looking for the answers.

The risk that I choose to embrace is to encourage my students to discover questions.

Seeing students arrive at important questions is one of my greatest joys as a teacher.

A key question I have discovered is, "How can we dabble with ideas so frequently that we become increasingly equipped to detect important relationships?"

It just might be that the students who have developed the greatest number sense or language skills are the very same students who have developed the greatest repertoire of dabbling.

Dabbling with ideas is valuable in a variety of subject areas. Dabbling with ideas allows us to sort out what may or may not be useful in terms of deepening our learning. The very act of dabbling with ideas allows students to begin discovering questions. When students discover questions, they then begin to determine which questions are important. And during this discovery process, they will come to understand that while, yes, answers are important, *questions* can be extraordinary.

KEY QUESTIONS

1. How often do you step into a lesson with the intention of discovering a question?

2. Are your students primarily seeking answers, or are they focused on the discovery of questions?

3. What kinds of questions are worth discovering?

4. If you or your students discover a question during a lesson, how do you capture it and make sure that it remains available to the students?

5. What are some actions you can take that promote a classroom culture that values the discovery of questions?

CHAPTER 19
The Gift

In the summer of 2005, I was given one of the greatest gifts of my teaching career. It was a question.

"What is it that makes a truly great teacher?"

I was not expecting the question, and I vividly remember mentally reaching back into my experience as a student, identifying a teacher, and suddenly realizing the answer.

A great teacher may be an expert in content, but what makes a teacher truly great actually has very little to do with content. A truly great teacher causes you to see something amazing and important about yourself that you didn't even realize existed. He or she causes something within you to awaken. The teacher's belief in you causes you to believe in yourself. Suddenly you feel more capable and more powerful. Your very self-context expands in a way that you never imagined possible.

That question continues to challenge me as an educator. It causes me to wonder what impact I am having on my students. When I prepare lessons, I ask: Is my intention simply to teach students layer upon layer of content or am I striving to help them reach for and discover their boundless potential?

I never want my lessons to be about the content. I want my lessons to be all about the students who are learning the content. It is all about the students.

With that student-focused intention in mind, I posted the next Big Idea on the wall:

—— BIG IDEA 19 ——
Consider Your Strengths.

Introducing the Big Idea

"You are amazing learners. You have already become very good at many, many things. And there is so much more you want to learn. You can wait for me to give you ideas about what you can learn, or you can start by thinking about this: What are some things that you are already very good at? Maybe you are really good at helping others learn. That is a powerful strength because it helps you learn, too. Maybe you have become a very focused writer. That is another powerful strength because it helps you think.

"Now, I want you to think about something else. There may be something amazing about yourself, a strength you haven't even discovered yet. I want you to consider that for a moment...

"The truth is, there may be many, many strengths you haven't discovered yet. Just as you are discovering powerful, important questions, you may come to realize that you have some amazing, extraordinary strengths that you aren't even aware of yet. I want you to consider your strengths—both the ones that you know about now, and the ones that you are going to discover as you travel through your learning journey.

"Over the next weeks and months, I may be teaching a lesson that is focused on social studies, or science, or reading, or writing, but you may learn something far beyond what I am teaching. You may learn

something very powerful about yourself as a learner. Yes, I want you to learn the ideas that I am teaching, but I want you to keep an additional layer of learning in mind; I want you to consider your strengths. I want you to notice them. I want you to watch them grow. You are an amazing learner, and I want you to pay attention to what happens as you learn. You may learn something that is far more important than whatever I had planned on that day. So as we travel through our lessons together, I want you to do this: I want you to continually consider your strengths."

It is very interesting to note that when many people are asked to consider their strengths, they quickly contrast what they feel they are good at with those things they consider to be their weaknesses. When we consider our strengths, we very often simultaneously consider our weaknesses.

Additionally, many people assume that strengths and weaknesses are static. Some even come to the erroneous conclusion that it is impossible to improve in certain areas of their lives.

Big Idea 19 has nothing to do with weaknesses, and it has nothing to do with the false concept that strengths are fixed or static. It has everything to do with paying attention to your growth and watching what happens to your strengths as you permit yourself to question, to struggle, to succeed, to fail, and to reflect. With every experience we can all grow as learners, especially if we are hungry to recognize the impact of those experiences.

I do not expect my students to think of their strengths as something that could be identified during a one-time inventory. I expect them to daily consider their strengths and to fully anticipate that their strengths will grow and change as they do. By paying attention to how their strengths continue to evolve, they will recognize that they are learners—powerful learners—who can choose to pursue an enormous array of strengths and possibilities.

Notice that no part of this message communicates that students are destined to live within a limited range of strengths. The entire point is to encourage students to constantly notice how their strengths grow as they learn and to recognize that they are continually growing as powerful learners who can engage in struggle. Learning is not easy. It is usually messy, frequently difficult, often frustrating, and at the very same time it is empowering and exciting.

As students travel through the process, their awareness of their growing strengths empowers them to keep learning more about learning itself. They will understand that very often wrestling, struggling, and contending with ideas is at the heart of learning. One of the greatest strengths they can develop is the willingness to enter into risky territory and to grapple with new concepts.

The students' journeys, whether filled with successes or failures—or, more likely, filled with some of both—will feature a growing array of strengths. Among the many strengths within that array may be some strengths that were entirely unexpected by the students. They may discover something new, something that they did not even realize ever existed. As I struggle to improve as a teacher, I want my students to frequently and deeply consider their strengths.

How the Idea Grew

When I read the words, "Consider Your Strengths" on the wall of my classroom, two concepts quickly come to mind. The first one is about my current strengths. I wonder if any of my strengths can be advantageous to my students. If so, I want to maximize and leverage those strengths to the best of my ability for the benefit of my students.

The second concept is one that propels me forward. "Consider my strengths" makes me wonder what strengths I can discover within myself. I am certain that, exactly like my students, if I pay close attention to my personal learning journey, I will continue to see growth. Paying attention to that growth encourages me and helps me recognize the growth that comes when I willingly struggle with new concepts. My growth may be slow, or it may be rapid, but the willingness to consider my strengths—both those I see now and the ones I want to see in the future—and to enter into the struggle to grow is the key.

Within that struggle, I can encounter an important question: How can I turn a current risk into a future strength? How can I grow into a strength that feels like it is out of reach and then go on to stand on that new strength to reach for even more growth.

I am constantly considering my strengths, and I find that it helps me locate opportunities to take growth risks. When I take those risks, I grow. And that is exactly what I want my students to do.

How can I turn a current risk into a future strength?

KEY QUESTIONS

1. What happens when students realize that they have the ability to wrestle with a "weakness" and turn it into a strength?

2. How can we help students see their strengths as areas of continual growth?

3. What is a growth risk that you could choose to take, either publically or privately?

CHAPTER 20
BLAZING AHEAD

Many strengths are rapidly growing within a classroom learning community.
Our own learning journeys are brimming with discoveries, reflections, and questions. Those journeys constantly stretch forward. Sometimes we do not realize the intensity of our journey, and even when we do, we may not fully realize how much those around us are also growing.

Our experiences have an enormous capacity to contribute to the growth of others. However, we can become so absorbed by the challenges we face that we may forget to examine our experiences with the intent of determining how our discoveries can contribute to the lives of other learners.

That is exactly what I challenged my students to do.

BIG IDEA 20

WHEN YOU DISCOVER SOMETHING NEW, DESIGN A PATH THAT CAN BE FOLLOWED.

Introducing the Big Idea

"Girls and boys, when you learn something new, our classroom community becomes more powerful because of your learning—if we can find a way to share our learning with one another. I want to challenge you to start thinking about how to let your ideas help other people learn.

"I'm deeply interested in your ideas. I'm also very interested in the paths that you take to reach those ideas. Pay attention to your learning pathways. If you do, then you can share your ideas with others much more clearly, and that is helpful.

"Make it possible for others to explore your learning pathways. It's not always easy, but if you pay attention to your thinking as you travel, that thinking can be shared, and that may be exactly what is most helpful to other learners in our classroom.

"When you discover something new, see if you can design a path that others can follow toward that learning.

"In order to do that, you need to pay attention to your thinking while you are discovering."

How the Idea Grew

The intentional pursuit of strengths, coupled with seeking ways to contribute to the strengths of others, challenged me to think more widely about the education profession. Like many other educators, I am on a learning journey and am determined to dig deeply into all that I can learn about education. But I knew I could not keep my discoveries to myself.

The concept of finding a means to share my learning with other educators caused me to think about my discoveries on another level. Through a wide range of experiences, I came to realize a new determination within me, and I began stating it often: I am determined to find my learning by giving it away.

There are so many parts of my learning journey that I simply cannot fully develop if I do not attempt to share them with others. It is often in the sharing of my journey that I learn the most. Many points of learning become complete when they are given away.

If it is true that our learning deepens when we share it with others, then not only do I need to share what I have learned, I am compelled to spread the message that we need to be sharing with one another, mutually contributing to one another's craft. And here is the most powerful part of this process: by contributing to one another's craft we are actually contributing to our own growth. That means, as we reach out to share with others, our own students have increasingly better-equipped teachers.

> I am determined to find my learning by giving it away.

Sometimes schools have mechanisms in place for educators to share their learning with one another. Other times, finding opportunities to share requires blazing trails, taking risks, and creating opportunities that did not previously exist.

Some of those risks take us far outside of our comfort zones. Speaking at a conference, hitting "publish" on a first blog post, sending out the first tweet with an educational hashtag, and asking other educators (or parents) to come observe our teaching are all examples of the kinds of uncomfortable risks that can ultimately lead to the kinds of deep personal growth that would be difficult to attain otherwise.

Perhaps the risks that will deeply challenge you include finding ways to help your students transform their world, explosively connecting students and educators around the globe in a way that has not yet been seen, or committing to a radically outside-the-box idea that you have always known would benefit your students.

You may be able to design other, more comfortable pathways to share your learning with others. However, the point is that when you learn something new, sharing it with others makes that discovery much more powerful.

Here is the truth: just like your students, you are stunning.

You are amazing.

You have so many powerful strengths that you can choose to pursue.

What is the most glorious learning risk you could take?

Do it! Turn that risk into a strength, and then stand on that strength to reach for something even more amazing!

And when you do, design a path that others can follow. That pathway will contribute to the learning of others, and the very creation of the pathway will powerfully contribute to your own learning.

Your risk is waiting for you. And because you are determined to share your learning, every step you take into that risky territory can contribute to the lives of countless others.

Key Questions

1. What is something important that you are learning about right now?

2. What are you hungry to learn more about?

3. What are some avenues you could use to share your learning with others?

4. Looking around your classroom, what are some of the most common avenues students are using to share their learning with one another?

5. At what point in the learning process is learning ready to be shared?

6. What is the most glorious risk you could take?

CHAPTER 21
THE CURRENCY OF LEARNING

S tudent thinking is the currency of learning.
    When students articulately exchange their thinking, the economy of the classroom culture becomes strong and robust. The economy is even stronger when students deliberately capture, produce, and share their ideas.

When students create thinking examples *specifically for the purpose of exchanging their thinking,* the classroom becomes *rich.*

Allow me to show you a simple image, along with an example of a story that brings it to life.

Thinking is currency.

Imagine a student who is working with the question, "What is twenty divided by three?" and responds with the loops on this picture. Now, let's look more deeply into the intent.

The intent of the graphic is not solely to determine the quotient. A far more important intent is to produce an example that can be used to articulately exchange thinking with other students.

Talking about thinking after the thinking has taken place is vastly different than producing representations of thinking designed with the specific intention of sharing one's thinking. Knowing you will have the opportunity to explain your thinking to someone else causes you as a learner to anticipate the articulation of your thinking in a way that will personally connect with other learners.

Let's listen in to some of the discussion between two students who are pointing at the representation of thinking.

"Twenty divided by three is six groups, and there are two left over."

"Two what? Two circles, or two groups?"

"Two circles. These two." (The student points to the two black circles in the bottom right.)

"You drew an extra circle here. Why did you do that? That changes the number to twenty-one."

"Do you see how every loop has a group of three inside?"

"Yeah."

"And there are six loops with black circles?"

"Seven, if you count this one."

"True. But there weren't three circles to draw a loop around. There were only two. So I drew a third circle—but I made it look different than the others so we could tell it apart. The last loop shows that those last circles are not a complete group of three. They would need one more circle to make a whole group of three. So I drew what the group would need to make a whole group of three."

"Why did you do that?"

"I've been waiting for that question! What fraction of the last group is shaded in?"

"Okay … two out of three are black. Two-thirds are black."

"That's right. So this example shows that twenty divided by three is equal to six whole groups (pointing to the six whole groups) and two-thirds of another group. My example shows that twenty divided by three is equal to six and two-thirds. Do you want to try it?"

The second student draws twenty dots, loops them in a different way, draws an additional circle, re-examines the representation and writes six and two-thirds.

"Okay," the second student continues. "I have two more ideas to share."

Two more pieces of currency, produced by the second student, land on the table.

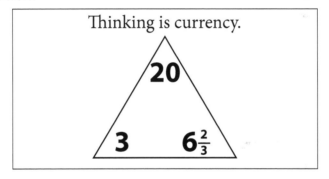

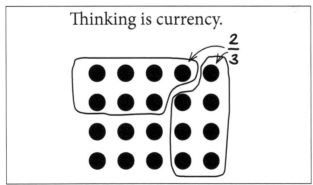

"The triangle shows how the three numbers are related. So twenty divided by six and two-thirds is equal to three. That means we can circle groups of six and two-thirds. There should be exactly three groups. This is my picture. Let me tell you what it means …"

The representations are built with the specific intent of sharing thinking with others.

The students are leading *by* example, and they are leading *with* examples.

BIG IDEA 21
LEAD BY EXAMPLE.

Introducing the Big Idea

"Boys and girls, we are going to learn about a new Big Idea today. 'Lead by Example.' I want each of you to lead others toward understanding your thinking. You can do that by creating examples that you can hold up and show to other people, examples that you can use to explain your thinking to other people. When you explain your thinking, you will be leading the learning of others, and your thinking will become even more powerful for you, too.

"My job will be to give you opportunities. Your job will be to lead. To do that, I want you to use examples of your thinking. I want you to lead by using examples.

"Lead by example."

How the Idea Grew

Representations of student thinking are instantly powerful. Yet I often felt as if something was missing from my classroom practice, something that I, initially, could not detect until I thought back to the old custom of show-and-tell. During weekly show-and-tell times, students brought their prized possessions to school so that they could show them to other students and tell all about them. Sometimes, students went on and on about the item they were so excited to share about.

In classrooms across the nation, teachers repeat the phrase, "Show your thinking." For example, I may often ask students to show their thinking on the page.

What is missing from that concept? It's the telling!

If I ask students to show their thinking, I may be communicating that I comprise the entire audience for the thinking. Furthermore, since they are showing their work on the paper, they may also come to believe that I am not necessarily planning to hear from them. After all, why would I need to? I have already asked them to show their thinking.

I am not as interested in having students show me their thinking as I am in having them show and tell others about their thinking. I want students to create thinking that is *intended for an audience and will be shared with an audience*. I'm not deeply interested in "Show your thinking." I'm enamored with "Show and tell your thinking." In the middle of the learning process, as students are making connections and producing meaning, I want them to anticipate that they will be sharing their current thinking with others.

It's worth noting that no element of perfection hovers near this concept. The point is simply for students to focus on thinking and to anticipate the articulation of that thinking. It is not about the artfulness of the representation. Students are free to tell about their thinking. They also begin to recognize the power of Big Idea 10 (We Learn from Our Successes), which previously seemed to be hiding in the glamorous shadow of Big Idea 9 (We Learn from Our Mistakes). Now the successes are shining through, and as those successes become the currency of the class, several of the other Big Ideas begin to deeply resonate.

In fact, if you look back through the list of Big Ideas, you may recognize that this single Big Idea has the potential to feature the power of nearly every other Big Idea we have discussed so far.

This very Big Idea, which sounds cliché upon first glance, actually has the power to serve as the hub of several other Big Ideas. An example is that when students build thinking representations, those representations can turn into the posterized thinking which I described in chapter 10, "We Learn from Our Successes."

The more closely I examine this concept, the more connections I discover to other Big Ideas. Making connections, making meaning, writing, valuing multiple pathways and multiple correct answers, constructing learning, leveraging mistakes and successes, building on what we know, encountering the impossible, discovering our potential, holding high expectations for ourselves as learners, growing our ideas, considering our strengths, and designing learning pathways that can be followed by others all intersect in powerful ways within the practice of "Lead by Example."

Further Growth over Time

Over the years, this idea has evolved significantly from its original intention, which was a generic phrase about leadership. How that well-worn phrase grew from a Big-Idea-in-Training into a powerful, central idea, I am not entirely sure. But the potential at its heart was this: build representations of your thinking that you will share with others. Then use those representations to explain your thinking. By doing so, your ideas will spread to others, and they will also become clearer to you, so you can wrestle with them even more. In addition, as ideas from many other learners multiply throughout the room, we will all become richer thinkers because of one another's ideas. The very act of sharing our own ideas will prepare us to understand others' ideas. We will all be leaders of learning. We will lead by sharing examples of our thinking.

I clearly remember that when I first placed this Big Idea on the wall, it felt like a risk. But I decided to take that risk, and it has paid off in ways that I never anticipated.

The act of sharing our own ideas will prepare us to understand others' ideas.

KEY QUESTIONS

1. Why is there such a profound difference between "Show your thinking" and "Show and tell your thinking?"

2. What is the effect on students when they see the thinking of other learners?

3. How difficult would it be to have students build examples of their thinking that are meant to be shared, rather than simply meant to be seen by the teacher? How would the representations themselves—or the time spent to create them—actually differ?

4. What steps would you need to take to establish the practice of exchanging ideas as richly as currency in your class?

5. How would you model this process in your classroom?

6. Why do you think this particular Big Idea intersects with so many other Big Ideas?

CHAPTER 22
"I Am Here to Learn!"

When I stepped into teaching, I was certain my students would be the ones who were going to learn.

Over time, I came to understand a very different truth.

Initially, I viewed the teacher as the one who already knows and the students as the ones who were about to learn the material that the teacher already knew. Clearly, this sounds like a transfer model.

The problem was that my model did not match the reality of classroom life. When I asked questions and listened—truly listened—to student responses, I discovered that their responses were not always what I was anticipating. In many cases, their responses were **better** than I had predicted. They saw ideas from multiple angles and used strategies that went beyond what I had expected. They posed points of view that illuminated my understanding.

My students amazed me—and they completely shattered my model. I was the teacher, but I was the one who was learning. And what were my students doing? They were teaching me! They were teaching one another.

Even though this realization did not happen in a single moment, when it finally occurred to me with clarity, I knew that my paradigm had to change.

I recognized this reality for years, before it finally occurred to me that I should publicly state this truth. I had thanked the students for helping me learn, I had given them strategies for helping one another learn, but I had not yet captured the concept with a Big Idea. During a year when I had 21 students, I attached Big Idea 22 to the wall.

BIG IDEA 22
22 Teachers, 22 Learners.

Introducing the Big Idea

"Girls and boys, today I have another Big Idea that I would like to share with you: '22 Teachers, 22 Learners.' I know that my job is to be the teacher and that your role is to be the students. But I want us to think about those roles in a new way. There are twenty-two of us in the class-room, and every one of us knows many things that the rest of us do not. We all have ideas that we can share with each other. Every one of you has amazing ideas to share, and when you share those ideas, we all learn more. Each one of us needs to be a teacher. That means our classroom has twenty-two teachers.

"Our classroom also has twenty-two learners, and this is also very important. You may think that I am the teacher and that my job is to

teach. That's true, but I also want you to know that I am a learner. I learn as much as I can every day. Every time I teach a lesson, I set out to learn something new. I learn from books, I learn from studying, and I also learn from you. This classroom is a great place for me to learn. Even though I am the teacher, I walk into class every day planning to learn as much as I possibly can. I have come here today to learn, and I am excited about it. I am ready to learn!"

With this single Big Idea, I had given myself a new public permission to no longer be the lone and perfect authoritative source of knowledge in the classroom. Even though I came to class as prepared as possible, anticipating student thinking and preparing lessons that were as effective as I knew how to make them, I also came with something else—something that was far more useful. I came with the public intention to be a learner.

Fundamentally, being a classroom learner allowed me to change my modeling, and it allowed me to demonstrate enthusiasm for learning at an entirely new level. Additionally, it allowed me to seek and share student thinking in entirely new ways that openly amazed me and set my students free as well. Suddenly, they eagerly looked for ways of thinking that would truly and authentically inspire their teacher.

From that day forward, I began each day by saying something I would never have said prior to posting Big Idea 22: "I have come to school today to learn as much as I possibly can. I am ready to learn, and I can't wait to find out what I will discover today! Thank you for helping me to learn." Then I would dive into the day ready to learn.

It is worth noting that this idea pushed my teaching to new places. I discovered that the questions asked by a teacher who is hungrily learning are far different than questions asked by a teacher with a transfer mindset.

With the public mindset of a learner, I provided my students with a clear opportunity to be producers of novel ideas. In fact, I expected students to think in new ways and to articulate their thinking clearly with the classroom community. Coming prepared for lessons gained an additional meaning to me. In addition to lesson preparation, it meant that I came prepared to detect the student thinking that could enrich the classroom community as a whole, and the students responded in impressive ways.

When I intentionally became a learner, I found that I was far better positioned to truly detect student thinking. After all, I was now searching for it. While this seems like a highly apparent truth, it was not plain to me until I experienced it. I am not sure I was even prepared to experience it *until* I shifted my stance to become a classroom learner.

The point was no longer to teach my thinking to the students so they would have thinking that matched mine. Instead, I was seeking thinking that was different than mine, thinking that would illuminate the understanding of the classroom community. It was easy to detect because it was unique, caused dissonance when set against current understandings, and called out for clear discourse that would allow us to understand those ideas.

I now recognize that when I intentionally enter the classroom as both a teacher and a learner, my role as a learner contributes to my personal and professional growth and is a tremendous asset to my students. I am determined to be a learner.

How the Idea Grew

Today, when I see "22 Teachers, 22 Learners" posted on the wall, I am quickly reminded that my role is not to compartmentalize teachers from learners. I am reminded that, when I learn something new or struggle to learn something new during the school day, I need to point that out to the students. My struggles are immensely important to my students because they provide an opportunity for me to share how I work through them, and many times wrestling with new learning is exactly what the students need to see.

Come to class every day hungry to learn.

In many ways, I have moved from being a teacher who never wanted to publicly struggle to one who openly welcomes struggle.

One of the roles I intentionally strive for is to be a living model of learning for my students. When they look up and see me, I do not want them to merely see a person who knows a set of ideas, skills, and strategies that I will share with them. Instead, I want my students to see someone who is modeling a passionate pursuit of learning. It is not always pretty, and it is never perfect, but it is highly intentional.

One of the roles that I intentionally strive for is to be a living model of learning for my students.

Every one of us is on a learning journey. Positioning ourselves as experts can partially cap our willingness to learn new ideas, hamper our willingness to take risks, and impede our eagerness to venture into new territory. I challenge you to share your learning journey with your students. Allow them to see your growth, your intention, and your passion. Allow your journey to impact your students—and prepare to be impacted by them.

I am not an expert who is nearing the end of my journey. Instead, I choose to be a learner with visible momentum.

KEY QUESTIONS

1. How do you define your role as a teacher?

2. How do you define your students' roles?

3. In what ways do you model learning in front of your students?

4. How overtly have you communicated your role as a learner with your students?

CHAPTER 23
The Inspiration Privilege

O ne of the clearest lessons I have learned as a teacher is to anticipate inspiration. I am not talking about any inspiration that could come from me. The students are the ones who inspire. They are creative, stunning, and full of surprises! Working with students is an enormous privilege.

BIG IDEA 23
Anticipate Inspiration.

Introducing the Big Idea

"I want to say something that is very important for you to hear. Thank you! Thank you for the privilege of coming to school every day and learning with you and learning from you. You put me in awe. I am very, very fortunate to learn with you. My job is called teacher, but I think it should be called Fortunate Learner.

"As you travel through your learning journey, I want you to look for moments of learning that come from other people. Sometimes you'll experience those moments at school, but much of the time it happens outside of school. You may hear ideas or see examples in other people that contribute to your lives.

"I plan to contribute to your lives each and every day. That is part of my job. But I want you to look beyond what I share with you. I want you to anticipate—or expect ahead of time—moments that will surprise you. Doesn't it sound funny to expect surprises? But that is exactly what I want you to do. I want you to be prepared to detect powerful learning moments that might have otherwise passed you by.

"Let me give you an example. The example is you. Your thinking is so powerful, so amazing, and so striking that I learn from you every single day. Yet, I could somehow overlook it if I wasn't paying attention. So I am determined to pay attention. I am determined to anticipate. I am determined to recognize—the best I can—that you inspire me every single day.

"Thank you!

"I know that I am very, very fortunate to learn from you. But in order to do that, I have to make a choice to pay attention to what you have to teach me. That's why I choose to anticipate. I choose to anticipate inspiration."

This Big Idea has very little do with the way teachers inspire their students.

This Big Idea is about how inspiring the students can be to their teachers and to one another.

When I walk into a classroom anticipating inspiration, I am not expecting to be the one to inspire the students. Rather, I am fully expecting to be inspired *by the students*. I also fully understand that one of the deepest sources of inspiration for each of the students may not be me. Instead, the students may best be inspired *by one another*.

How the Idea Grew

When I entered the teaching profession, the concept of seeking to be inspired by the students did not occur to me. I was focused on teaching the students—focused on teaching content to the students.

As the years progressed, I learned to give the students more and more space in the learning process. I learned to move away from what was quantifiable, and to step into some riskier territory. Prior to this learning, I understood how to correct a page of twenty questions, write a percentage correct on the top of the page, and to partially gauge the success of the lesson for each student based on that score. However, those questions usually had answers that could be scored, that could be graded, and that could be referenced to an answer key.

While there is a very important place for efficiency, and more importantly, for a way to gauge each student's level of understanding with important foundational skills, it is imperative to understand that, if it is carried too far, that place can be very limiting to both students and teachers.

If the greatest latitude I give to students is to be able to produce answers that have already been discovered by someone else and have already been printed in an answer key, how much am I really allowing them to grow? In such a case, students may become successful on objective after objective after objective and still gain very little ground as learners.

It is difficult to be inspired as a teacher if the goal, day after day, is merely for students to produce work that matches an existing answer key.

When this realization occurred to me, I began adapting my lessons so that they provided much more space for students to think. And within that thinking space, the students amazed me. They inspired me.

Now I anticipate inspiration.

I give the students space to stun me.

Let me tell you that this process was not easy. It was not painless, and it was not fast. Sometimes we struggled, wrestled, ran into very difficult obstacles and had no idea how to go forward. That does not sound very inviting does it?

But listen to that sentence again in the context of providing a powerful learning experience for students: "Sometimes we struggled, wrestled, ran into very difficult obstacles and had no idea how to go forward." That is precisely the place where learning becomes powerful.

> **Not only do I need to anticipate inspiration, I need to give the students opportunities to rise above profound challenges.**

That is the risk that I want to take, and it is the place where I want my students to return day after day. It is also precisely the point from which students inspire me as they rise above worthwhile challenges.

Not only do I need to anticipate inspiration, I need to give the students opportunities to rise above profound challenges. Yes, those challenges can frighten me. What happens if they do not rise above them? What if they fail? What if I fail?

The truth is that those struggles are okay. It is important to face profound challenges that we do not yet know how to conquer. Being willing to face deep challenges, rather than avoiding them, is a critical part of our journey.

I am looking for inspiration. I am anticipating inspiration, and I fully recognize that it may not come from me at all. The students are amazing, and I stand in awe. I also stand in anticipation of inspiration.

KEY QUESTIONS

1. Are you providing space for your students to inspire you?

2. Who inspires whom in the classroom?

3. Are there some simple adjustments you can make to give your students more room to inspire you and to inspire one another?

CHAPTER 24
Just Beginning

N o matter how many Big Ideas are posted on the wall, there is always room to add one more. This one. It is an invitation. It is also a charge to both myself and my students.

─────── BIG IDEA 24 ───────
Discover a Big Idea.

Introducing the Big Idea

"Girls and boys, I have so much more to learn. We all do. The class-room is only one place where our learning happens. This Big Idea says, 'Discover a Big Idea.' This is an invitation to keep looking for Big Ideas, important ideas, ideas that help us to learn more about learning itself. When we think we find one, we'll add it to the wall.

"We have shared several Big Ideas together, but there are more. They are waiting to be discovered. As you learn important ideas in the classroom, I want you to be thinking about even bigger learning. I want you to look for Big Ideas in your life. Seek them out. Discover them. Capture them.

"Learning may be about small skills. It is also about Big Ideas. I want you to learn about your learning. I want you to notice, to pay attention, to write your ideas down, and to think about them deeply. You may discover something very important that nobody else has yet thought about. Look for the Big Ideas. Discover them. I challenge you to discover a Big Idea."

Key Questions

1. Are there any Big Ideas in this book that might fit nicely on your classroom wall?

2. Is there a concept that is not mentioned in this book that could potentially become a Big Idea in your classroom?

3. What learning verb would you like to see your students more fully activate in your classroom?

4. If you were to choose one Big Idea from the book to post on your wall, which one would you begin with?

5. What do you think may be the most important Big Idea in this book?

THE IDEAS
THAT FELL
OFF THE WALL

The Big Ideas literally fell off of the wall every time there was a noticeable change in the weather that caused the classroom heater to come on overnight. As winter pressed on, I would arrive at school early in the morning, often to find that some Big Idea posters were dangling from a single corner by a valiant piece of tape while others had fluttered to the floor.

At first, it was frustrating to keep fixing the ideas back on the wall, but it eventually caused me to wonder, "Is this idea worth keeping on the wall? Is it important enough that I post it every day?"

There were several Big Ideas that appeared briefly on our wall but did not survive over time. They were important for a season but did not appear to have a profound, lasting truth that had the potential to daily impact our classroom community.

Many Big Ideas came and went. Every single idea that appeared on the wall was important. Even the ones that seemed important but faded out later helped us learn something useful.

The ideas that came and went do not appear in this book.

However, among the many Big Ideas that are detailed in this book, there are two that nearly fell off of the wall right away, but ended up being useful for different reasons. Big Idea 2 and Big Idea 3 were nearly taken down.

Big Idea 2: Addition and Subtraction Are Connected.

Big Idea 3: Multiplication and Division Are Connected.

Big Idea 2, in particular, never truly became part of our classroom culture. It was a content-based example that did not seem to speak a lot of truth into the messages that I communicated to my students. However, its practicality seemed to ground the other ideas, especially early in the journey. There were several winter mornings when I found this idea on the floor and was tempted to not reattach it to the wall. Yet, it seemed to hold a different kind of importance because of its history with Big Idea 1 and the fact that it was the idea that truly started the momentum. So it stayed on the wall as part of the story.

Big Idea 3 nearly came down for a similar reason. It seemed too specific. However, the more we studied multiplication, division, fractions, decimals, ratios, and other mathematical concepts, the more profound this idea became. It seemed to work especially well in combination with other Big Ideas, such as Big Idea 17, which encouraged us to grow our ideas.

Even though these two ideas dangled tentatively for a time, they eventually found a very solid place on the wall for reasons that were different than the others.

How to Keep the Ideas Attached to the Wall

The fact that some of the ideas literally fell off of the wall—and the fact that I had to keep reattaching them to the wall—led me to ask some important questions. What is it that keeps a Big Idea attached to the fabric of our learning community? And how can I keep the Big Ideas attached to the classroom community which they are intended to serve?

The answer is quite simple. Refer to them. Mention them often. Point to them. Weave them into the fabric of the conversation. Then listen.

The Big Ideas that easily and naturally find their way into discussions in the classroom, with parents, with groups of students, and with individuals, are the ones that are becoming firmly affixed to the fabric of the classroom culture. The Big Ideas that are part of the classroom dialogue are the Big Ideas that remain firmly attached to the learning journey.

When a student says, "I just learned from my success. I went back and looked at my thinking and I discovered something new ..."

Or "I already knew the answer, but I wanted to go back and find another pathway ..."

Or "I remember when that seemed to be impossible ..."

Or "I just grew my idea ..."

Or even when a student simply reaches for a journal at an unexpected time during a lesson and begins writing, I know that these Big Ideas have become firmly attached to my students' hearts and minds.

The Big Ideas that are seldom mentioned or demonstrated start to slip off the wall. When a Big Idea begins to metaphorically dangle by the last corner of meaningful attachment to the wall, then its purpose may be nearly complete for the time being. It is perfectly fine to take it off the wall. I have learned that I do not have to wait for another Big Idea to replace it. I do not have to take it down ceremoniously. I can simply remove it.

But which ideas survive the test of time? If you review the Big Ideas in this book, you will notice that they all speak directly to the concept of learning, directly to the assets of learning, or directly to the learner. The ideas that open opportunities for us to learn more about learning itself stay strongly affixed to the wall of our classroom culture. Those ideas pass a simple test: Big Ideas worth keeping help us to learn about learning, and they help us to learn about ourselves as learners.

2007

In June of 2007, I moved to a new school district. The time had come for me to take the Big Ideas off of the wall that they had lived on for so long. Carefully, I took them down and packed them up along with the many items I had accumulated during my first twelve years of teaching. For many reasons, moving out of a classroom is an emotional, draining experience.

Behind me, I left an empty wall.

Several weeks later, as I stepped into my new classroom, I took some time to simply look around, to take it in. So much was new to me, and I had a great deal to learn. But that was not what was on my mind.

I was scanning the walls, and I quickly found it. There it was. The perfect space.

The Blank Space on Your Classroom Wall

There is a blank space on your classroom wall right now. If you look around your room, you will find it. It is waiting for you to fill it with an important message. It is waiting for you to fill it with a Big Idea. What would you like to write in that space?

As you near the end of this book, I have a challenge for you. Like many of the Big Ideas I have presented here, the challenge is both simple and profound. I encourage you to actively seek out both of those layers in this challenge.

I challenge you to post at least one Big Idea on your classroom wall, to teach your students what it means, to let that idea challenge you personally, and then to share your experience with fellow educators.

To help with this process, I have detailed seven key steps below.

1. Select an important idea.

Choose a single idea. It does not have to be deeply profound, and it certainly does not have to be perfect. Waiting for perfection before you ever share is not an idea that you want to promote with your students, and it is the surest pathway to never sharing your own ideas. Simply select what you feel is an important idea that you can learn from. Don't worry if it doesn't feel "big enough." It is just beginning. It has not had time to grow yet. You are testing it out. There will be plenty of time and space to choose other ideas. Just start with one. If you want, take one of the ideas that I have included in this book. You can simply flip back through the pages and choose one that resonates with you.

2. Post it on your classroom wall.

Give it a place of prominence in your classroom. Make sure that it is clearly in view and constantly available for students so that you can quickly refer to it in the thick of instruction. If possible, keep it within the students' line of sight, so they can refer to it as well. Give them a clear opportunity to amaze you with their insights.

3. Explain to your students what the Big Idea means to you.

If you have chosen an idea that you feel is complex, profound, or multi-layered, you may feel that it is too complicated for students to grasp. Do not let this stop you. Students are amazing, astonishing learners. Learning—for all of us—involves a journey. What matters is that we begin the journey. You will refer to this idea often, and it will become much more powerful over time. You will have many chances to unwrap the complexity of the idea with your students. It is not necessary that you try to fully uncover all of the power of the idea when you first present it. Even you will not be aware of how significant the idea may eventually become. Simply set it in motion by explaining what it means to you.

4. Be prepared to let the idea impact you personally.

Be a learner. Live the learning. Actively pursue connections. You chose the idea for a reason, so it has your attention, and you are ready to learn from it. As you journey, pay attention to your own learning and do not be afraid to tell your students about that learning. Your shared learning experiences may be precisely what will ignite the power of the Big Idea in your classroom. Do not think that the idea is only for the students. Such an approach would immediately limit the impact of the idea. Step into the journey, knowing that you may soon be sharing reflections of how the idea has impacted you. Your modeling will pave the way for students to share how the idea is impacting them.

5. Seek opportunities to feature the idea.

Look for moments of opportunity. For example, if the idea you have posted is "Learning Is about Making Connections" and a student makes a powerful connection in class, quickly mention, "Nice connection. Learning is about making connections." Or when you find a connection, you can say, "I just made a connection." Prefacing statements with Big Ideas can quickly embed the ideas into the conversation and, eventually, into the fabric of your classroom culture.

6. Grow your set of Big Ideas.

As you continue through the school year, look for further Big Ideas that you can add to your wall. Again, you are welcome to take the Big Ideas that have already been presented in this book, or you can find ones that are tailored to your classroom community. Post them prominently, explain them, and allow them to grow into your classroom culture. Do not be surprised if students or parents propose Big Ideas. Also, do not be surprised if you try a Big Idea and it simply falls flat. That is part of the learning experience. Do not wait for perfection. Pursue the possible and see what happens. Sometimes removing a Big Idea is part of the process.

7. Share your Big Ideas.

This is a critical step, not to be overlooked. While your Big Ideas emerge within the context of your classroom community and will carry the greatest meaning within the community that experiences them together, do not forget the importance of sharing and discussing those ideas with other educators. Sharing your ideas will offer you powerful opportunities to learn from them.

When you share your ideas with others, your classroom community will benefit. You will gain additional insights and you will likely receive a multitude of perspectives that otherwise would never have occurred to you. Sharing your ideas is a significant growth step that will deeply impact you and will reach into your classroom community, where it will further benefit your students.

Share with a mentor, share with another teacher who is using Big Ideas, or share with your staff. If you are presenting at a conference, choose one or two Big Ideas to weave into your presentation. Share your journey.

I also encourage you to share your ideas with other educators around the world using social media and digital platforms. Join the ongoing conversation on Twitter at #TWOTCW (The Writing on the Classroom Wall).

Sharing your ideas will sharpen and refine them. You will discover that when a new school year begins, you will be ready to share several Big Ideas right away with your new class. In that moment, a new classroom community will begin to emerge, and it will be informed by the experiences of the students from the year before. Likewise, your new set of students will have experiences that will eventually inform the group of students that you will work with the next year.

A New Learning Journey

You have a rich opportunity to begin a new learning journey. I challenge you to take the first steps. Choose a Big Idea, write it on your wall, and let the journey begin.

Give yourself permission to learn more about learning itself and to share that learning with your students. Then, when you are in the thick of instruction or are wondering deeply during a time of reflection, glance up at the space that used to be empty, the space that you chose to fill with a very important idea, and discover what you can learn from the writing on your classroom wall.

ACKNOWLEDGMENTS

The depth of my gratitude to the many educators and friends who have contributed directly to this book cannot be fully described. I would first like to offer my deep gratitude to Bonnie Van Cleave, Stephanie Knapp, Katy Creason, Cheri Clausen, and Hank Wyborney for their generous time and many insightful thoughts that contributed to this work.

I would also like to express many thanks to Erin Casey for her numerous contributions. I am determined to grow as a writer, and crossing paths with Erin has been an enormous blessing. Additionally, I am deeply grateful to Shelley Burgess and Dave Burgess for their belief in me.

Finally, I would like to express my greatest appreciation to Jeannine, Ben, and Natalie—my family who patiently supported my countless hours of writing.

MORE FROM

DAVE BURGESS
Consulting, inc.

Teach Like a PIRATE

*Increase Student Engagement, Boost Your
Creativity, and Transform Your Life as an Educator*
By Dave Burgess (@BurgessDave)

Teach Like a PIRATE is the New York Times'
best-selling book that has sparked a worldwide
educational revolution. It is part inspirational
manifesto that ignites passion for the profession
and part practical road map, filled with dynamic
strategies to dramatically increase student
engagement. Translated into multiple languages,
its message resonates with educators who want
to design outrageously creative lessons and transform school into a life-changing experience for students.

Learn Like a PIRATE

*Empower Your Students to Collaborate,
Lead, and Succeed*

By Paul Solarz (@PaulSolarz)

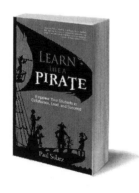

Today's job market demands that students be
prepared to take responsibility for their lives and
careers. We do them a disservice if we teach them
how to earn passing grades without equipping
them to take charge of their education. In Learn
Like a Pirate, Paul Solarz explains how to design
classroom experiences that encourage students
to take risks and explore their passions in a stim-
ulating, motivating, and supportive environment
where improvement, rather than grades, is the focus. Discover how student-led
classrooms help students thrive and develop into self-directed, confident citizens
who are capable of making smart, responsible decisions, all on their own.

P is for PIRATE

Inspirational ABC's for Educators

By Dave and Shelley Burgess (@Burgess_Shelley)

Teaching is an adventure that stretches the imagination and calls for creativity every day! In *P is for Pirate*, husband and wife team, Dave and Shelley Burgess, encourage and inspire educators to make their classrooms fun and exciting places to learn. Tapping into years of personal experience and drawing on the insights of more than seventy educators, the authors offer a wealth of ideas for making learning and teaching more fulfilling than ever before.

Play Like a Pirate

Engage Students with Toys, Games, and Comics

by Quinn Rollins

Yes! School can be simultaneously fun and educational. In *Play Like a Pirate*, Quinn Rollins offers practical, engaging strategies and resources that make it easy to integrate fun into your curriculum. Regardless of the grade level you teach, you'll find inspiration and ideas that will help you engage your students in unforgettable ways.

eXPlore Like a Pirate

Gamification and Game-Inspired Course Design to Engage, Enrich, and Elevate Your Learners

By Michael Matera (@MrMatera)

Are you ready to transform your classroom into an experiential world that flourishes on collaboration and creativity? Then set sail with classroom game designer and educator, Michael Matera, as he reveals the possibilities and power of game-based learning. In *eXPlore Like a Pirate*, Matera serves as your experienced guide to help you apply the most motivational techniques of gameplay to your classroom. You'll learn gamification strategies that will work with and enhance (rather than replace) your current curriculum and discover how these engaging methods can be applied to any grade level or subject.

Pure Genius

*Building a Culture of Innovation and
Taking 20% Time to the Next Level*

By Don Wettrick (@DonWettrick)

For far too long, schools have been bastions of boredom, killers of creativity, and way too comfortable with compliance and conformity. In *Pure Genius*, Don Wettrick explains how collaboration—with experts, students, and other educators—can help you create interesting, and even life-changing, opportunities for learning. Wettrick's book inspires and equips educators with a systematic blueprint for teaching innovation in any school.

The Zen Teacher

*Creating FOCUS, SIMPLICITY, and TRANQUILITY in
the Classroom*

By Dan Tricarico (@TheZenTeacher)

Teachers have incredible power to influence, even improve, the future. In *The Zen Teacher*, educator, blogger, and speaker, Dan Tricarico, provides practical, easy-to-use techniques to help teachers be their best—unrushed and fully focused—so they can maximize their performance and improve their quality of life. In this introductory guide, Dan Tricarico explains what it means to develop a Zen practice—something that has nothing to do with religion and everything to do with your ability to thrive in the classroom.

Master the Media

*How Teaching Media Literacy Can
Save Our Plugged-in World*

By Julie Smith (@julnilsmith)

Written to help teachers and parents educate the next generation, *Master the Media* explains the history, purpose, and messages behind the media. The point isn't to get kids to unplug; it's to help them make informed choices, understand the difference between truth and lies, and discern perception from reality. Critical thinking leads to smarter decisions—and it's why media literacy can save the world.

The Innovator's Mindset

Empower Learning, Unleash Talent,
and Lead a Culture of Creativity

By George Couros (@gcouros)

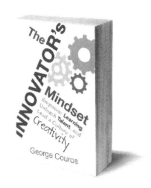

The traditional system of education requires students to hold their questions and compliantly stick to the scheduled curriculum. But our job as educators is to provide new and better opportunities for our students. It's time to recognize that compliance doesn't foster innovation, encourage critical thinking, or inspire creativity—and those are the skills our students need to succeed. In *The Innovator's Mindset*, George Couros encourages teachers and administrators to empower their learners to wonder, to explore—and to become forward-thinking leaders.

50 Things You Can Do with Google Classroom

By Alice Keeler and Libbi Miller
(@AliceKeeler, @MillerLibbi)

It can be challenging to add new technology to the classroom, but it's a must if students are going to be well-equipped for the future. Alice Keeler and Libbi Miller shorten the learning curve by providing a thorough overview of the Google Classroom App. Part of Google Apps for Education (GAfE), Google Classroom was specifically designed to help teachers save time by streamlining the process of going digital. Complete with screenshots, *50 Things You Can Do with Google Classroom* provides ideas and step-by-step instructions to help teachers implement this powerful tool.

140 Twitter Tips for Educators

Get Connected, Grow Your Professional
Learning Network, and Reinvigorate Your Career

By Brad Currie, Billy Krakower, and Scott Rocco
(@bradmcurrie, @wkrakower, @ScottRRocco)

Whatever questions you have about education or about how you can be even better at your job, you'll find ideas, resources, and a vibrant network of professionals ready to help you on Twitter. In *140 Twitter Tips for Educators*, #Satchat hosts and founders of Evolving Educators, Brad Currie, Billy Krakower, and Scott Rocco offer step-by-step instructions to help you master the basics of Twitter, build an online following, and become a Twitter rock star.

Ditch That Textbook

*Free Your Teaching and Revolutionize
Your Classroom*

By Matt Miller (@jmattmiller)

Textbooks are symbols of centuries of old education. They're often outdated as soon as they hit students' desks. Acting "by the textbook" implies compliance and a lack of creativity. It's time to ditch those textbooks—and those textbook assumptions about learning! In *Ditch That Textbook*, teacher and blogger Matt Miller encourages educators to throw out meaningless, pedestrian teaching and learning practices. He empowers them to evolve and improve on old, standard teaching methods. *Ditch That Textbook* is a support system, toolbox, and manifesto to help educators free their teaching and revolutionize their classrooms.

Your School Rocks...So Tell People!

*Passionately Pitch and Promote the
Positives Happening on Your Campus*

By Ryan McLane and Eric Lowe
(@McLane_Ryan, @EricLowe21)

Great things are happening in your school every day. The problem is: no one beyond your school walls knows about them. School principals Ryan McLane and Eric Lowe want to help you get the word out! In *Your School Rocks...So Tell People!*, McLane and Lowe offer more than seventy immediately actionable tips along with easy-to-follow instructions and links to video tutorials. This practical guide will equip you to create an effective and manageable communication strategy using social media tools. Learn how to keep your students' families and community connected, informed, and excited about what's going on in your school.

How Much Water Do We Have?

5 Success Principles for Conquering Any
Change and Thriving in Times of Change

by Pete Nunweiler with Kris Nunweiler

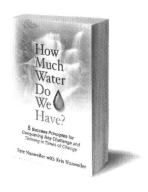

In *How Much Water Do We Have?* Pete Nunweiler identifies five key elements—information, planning, motivation, support, and leadership—that are necessary for the success of any goal, life transition, or challenge. Referring to these elements as the 5 Waters of Success, Pete explains that like the water we drink, you need them to thrive in today's rapidly paced world. If you're feeling stressed out, overwhelmed, or uncertain at work or at home, pause and look for the signs of dehydration. Learn how to find, acquire, and use the 5 Waters of Success—so you can share them with your team and family members.

The Classroom Chef

Sharpen your lessons. Season your classes.
Make math meaningful.

By John Stevens and Matt Vaudrey
(@Jstevens009, @MrVaudrey)

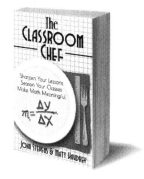

In *The Classroom Chef*, math teachers and instructional coaches, John Stevens and Matt Vaudrey, share their secret recipes, ingredients, and tips for serving up lessons that engage students and help them "get" math. You can use these ideas and methods as-is, or better yet, tweak them and create your own enticing educational meals. The message the authors share is that, with imagination and preparation, every teacher can be a Classroom Chef.

BRING BIG IDEAS
TO YOUR SCHOOL!

Steve Wyborney is a popular professional-development speaker who engages and inspires audiences.

Some of his most-requested sessions include...

The Writing on the Classroom Wall

High-Engagement Math Strategies for the Elementary Classroom

Using Animated Thinking Models to Promote Mathematical Discourse

To inquire about speaking engagements, contact Steve directly.

stevewyborney@gmail.com

SteveWyborney.com

@stevewyborney

ABOUT THE AUTHOR

Steve Wyborney stepped into his first classroom in the fall of 1995. Since that time, Steve has been a classroom teacher, a building instructional coach, a district math coach, and has spent six years as a looping teacher. Steve was named the 2005 Oregon Teacher of the Year, has received the L. E. Wesche Outstanding Educator Award, and was a national finalist for the Kinder Excellence in Teaching Award.

Steve frequently presents at conferences, and eagerly shares his learning, tools, and strategies with fellow educators. He is well-known for his passion for mathematics, instructional technology, and writing.

You can connect with Steve on his blog at SteveWyborney.com where he discusses topics about which he is hungry to learn more. He especially enjoys listening carefully and learning from educators around the world through the discussions on his blog and on Twitter @stevewyborney. One of the most recent Big Ideas that Steve has posted on his wall reads: "Listen. Listen More. Listen More Deeply."

Made in the USA
Middletown, DE
11 April 2019